The
Affable
CURMUDGEON

The
Affable
CURMUDGEON

Robert Vickrey

Drawings By
ED SMITH

PARNASSUS IMPRINTS
Orleans, Massachusetts

to Jeanne + Ron

Robert Vickrey

To
MARJORIE

A Wonderful Wife — and the
World's Greatest Straightman

CONTENTS

INTRODUCTION
THE MAKING OF A CURMUDGEON

O NE of my favorite *New Yorker* cartoons shows a grumpy man at a bar.
Someone next to him whispers to a friend, "He's a curmudgeon *now*, but
he used to be just a mean old bastard."

We curmudgeons are proud of our exalted status. "Curmudgeons are
made, not born," we state. By a slow process of encrustation, we build our
armor against the inanities of our world. We glow with the inner misconception
of the fanatic who *knows* that he is right when everyone else is
wrong. This does not make us popular, but our strength is as the strength
of ten because our hearts are pure.

A few years ago I felt the need to put some of my more reasonable ideas
into print. I approached Mal Hobbs, owner and publisher of the *The Cape
Codder*.

"Hmm," he said, "It might be fun."

"I may step on a few toes," I said.

"We've been sued a few times, but we've never lost," he said firmly,
"We need a little controversy. Just hand one in every couple of weeks."

A short time later my first article appeared.

"That's one of the funniest things I ever read," said Tom.

"Who wrote it for you?" said Dick.

"I enjoyed your short story," said Harry.

"It's not a short story," I said, "It's all true."

"Sure, sure," said Harry, patronizingly.

"I think you better stick to painting," said Jane.

I received letters, phone calls, postcards. Strangers stopped me on the street. I was very pleased. Some people began to say they liked my articles better than my paintings. I was *not* so pleased.

"How about describing some of your *Time* covers?" said Mal.

"Aren't you afraid of being sued by people like Kim Novak?" asked Tom.

"I send everything to a lawyer first," I said.

"Why don't you write about something serious," said my wife Marjorie, "Something like Fascism."

"In Orleans?" I asked.

"It's everywhere," she said.

I submitted some off-beat material to Mal, making fun of a pretentious local restaurant. He chuckled appreciatively, "We may lose some advertising, but so what! By the way, I'd like you to meet your new editor. Bob, this is Pru Dent. She's in charge of the Arts and Leisure section of our paper."

"Hi," I said to the likeable young woman who came into the office. "I have another article here. You may not want to print it. It's about the fact that I use condoms as bottle tops for my paint."

"We'll have to think that one over," said Mal, sobering.

"You'll never get that one through," said Tom later.

"Pru grew up in a painting by Norman Rockwell," said Dick.

"Ninety percent of the paper's income is from advertising," said Harry.

"Why don't you go back to painting?" said Jane.

"That . . . bottle top piece is the best thing you've ever done," said Tom.

"I'm collecting your stuff and sending it to people in the hospital to cheer them up," said Dick.

"Now I *really* like your articles better than your painting," said Harry.

"They're not for me," said Jane.

"Write about something serious," said Marjorie.

"O.K.," I said, "I'll write about Cape Cod's dreadful water."

"They won't print it," said my son Sean, "Four generations of Cape Codders want *that* kept a secret. You can't go up against *them*."

"I'll write it in the style of Jonathan Swift," I said.

"This is very funny," chuckled Mal later as he read the manuscript in my presence, "We just might *do* it."

"They'll never do it," cautioned my son Sean.

"The water is turning everything in our house brown and green," moaned Marjorie.

Months passed.

"I told you," said Sean.

I handed in several more articles.

"What about my water piece?" I asked Pru.

"Mal hasn't read it yet," she replied.

"But he read a lot of it right in front of me," I said.

I got a letter from Mal saying, "It doesn't make it as Swiftian satire."

"I'll rewrite it in the present," I said on the phone.

"Then it wouldn't be funny," he said.

"I'll make it funny."

"Look, I won't print *anything* you write about the water department in *any* style."

"Then it isn't the Swiftian style that bothers you."

"I gotta go," said Mal.

"You know what you should do," said my lawyer, "Condense your articles and send them as letters to the editor."

I did so. I also refused to pay my water bill until the water department admitted that the acid and iron in Cape Cod water were eating away copper pipes and destroying linen.

"You know," said Tom, "This is a very conservative publication. They even object to the Boston papers printing hurricane warnings for the Cape."

"Yeah," said Dick, "They once refused to write about a murder in town because it might hurt business."

"This *is* Norman Rockwell country," said Harry.

I thought of a possible 14 1/2 hour mini-series:

"Kape Kod! It opens with a Fourth of July parade. We see banners of George Washington, Abraham Lincoln, and Norman Rockwell. There are rumors that a hydrogen bomb has destroyed Provincetown, but the local paper won't mention it because it might hurt business . . ."

"Your condom article doesn't exactly have me rolling in the aisle, but Mal says to print it," read a letter from Pru.

"You know," said my lawyer a few weeks later, "You should get donations from the hundreds of people who agree with you and *buy* a full page ad in the paper to tell the truth about Cape Cod water."

I broached *this* idea to Mal. He finally agreed to print my article. "As long as it's funny," he added.

"They actually published it?" asked Tom.

"I see that your stuff is coming out all over the country now," said Dick.

"Don't expect to get too many articles printed in Orleans from now on, though," said Harry.

"Why don't you go back to painting?" said Jane.

"Or write about national politics," said Marjorie.

I wrote about painting LBJ, JFK, Pat Nixon, Tip O'Neill, and others.

"You've had too much publicity lately," said Pru, "We've decided to give you a cooling off period."

"But you've had some of these pieces for two years!" I protested.

"I told you so," said Tom.

"They *do* print them once in a while, though," said Dick.

"But," I added, "Now they're eliminating final paragraphs, taking out titles, and cutting off the punchlines."

"Are you surprised?" asked Harry.

"Why don't you . . . oh, what the hell," said Jane.

"I passed your last piece on to Mal," said Pru a few months later, "But he seems to have lost it."

"But that was my *only* copy," I groaned.

"Too bad!" she said cheerfully. "You know, if your pieces upset *anyone* in the entire world, we won't print them."

"What's left to write about?" I asked.

"Curmudgeons *are* made, not born," said Tom.

"Welcome to the club," said Dick.

"Maybe you can get someone to publish them in a book," suggested Harry.

"I doubt it," I said, "Who would be that crazy?"

A CHRISTMAS TO REMEMBER

W E live in an Alfred Hitchcock world. Something strange and unnerving is always going on just beneath the placid surface of our lives.

For example, many years ago, before I was married, I lived in a fourth floor walk-up in New York City's Greenwich Village. One room (furnished) with kitchenette was $35. That included gas and electricity. It was also supposed to include heat, but quite often did not. I would leave the oven on with the door open to combat this problem. Once I tried this when there was a mouse inside feasting on crumbs. He waited quietly inside until the heat became too intense for him. When pain overcame timidity, he scuttled briefly, then shot through the air across my line of vision in a perfect ten-foot parabola.

In those days I used to paint until dawn while listening to Symphony Sid on the radio. Occasionally, to break the monotony, I would play (at a very low level) Stravinsky's *Rite of Spring* or Walt Disney's *Songs From Snow White* on the phonograph. They were the only records I owned.

I never paid much attention to dates and holidays. One winter evening, while I was working on an apocalyptic vision of man's downfall, or some such other thing, I heard a timid knock on my door. When I opened it, there was no one in sight, but at my feet I saw a beribboned plate of cookies and a note which read:

"My daughter and I are alone on Christmas Eve, and we noticed that you are also. I hope your father is feeling better. Sincerely, Your Neighbor."

Who says that New Yorkers have no hearts? Still, I was worried about that reference to my father. Finally I realized that my telephone was right next to the wall between our two apartments. She must have been listening to my every word. I left a small drawing and a note of thanks outside her door. I also had the phone company install a *very* long extension cord. I

1

would take my phone into the bathroom and run the shower during all future conversations. A few days later I received another note attached to a little paper horn. It read:

"Happy New Year: My daughter and I are once again alone on a holiday. My son-in-law has left us, just as he does every night. I'm glad you're father is better."

I knew what my neighbor looked like from having seen her in the hall, so when I passed her on the stairs, I tried to start a friendly conversation.

No, no, she pantomined, looking around in terror. *He* might see us.

And she hurried away.

More notes arrived in the next few weeks:

"My son-in-law is poisoning my daughter. Every night he goes out and gets her a Coke at the drugstore. He brings it back in a container of ice. He won't allow us to keep Coke in the house. He must be putting something in her drink. My daughter is getting weaker and weaker. Don't try to contact me. *He* is always watching. I fear for my life.

"We like the Snow White music better than that horrible noisy stuff you play sometimes. Mr. Symphony is nice too.

"You should dress up more warmly on these cold nights."

Easter came . . . with a large bunny cookie and the usual missive:

"You must be as lonely as we are. I've found some small white pills hidden in the back of the medicine cabinet. They look like will-sapping pills to me. *He* must be slipping them into my daughter's Coke every night. She is now completely under his domination.

"You didn't look well the last time I saw you through our peephole. Are you getting enough to eat? Say hello to your girlfriend from us. I'm sorry that she has to be away for a while."

Eventually I spotted the fiend and his will-sapped wife on the stairs. They looked very innocent and happy. I searched the daughter/wife's eyes for lack of will.

More notes:

"Your girlfriend looks very nice. I think she should lose some weight, though. I'm glad that your father is back from Florida. He sounds like such a nice man.

"Why do you always talk on the telephone in the bathroom? How many showers a day do you take? It's not good to wash off all those protective layers. Have a nice 4th of July."

I was determined to stop her and offer to help, but she appeared more frightened than ever each time I tried.

"I can't go on," read the next communication. "We have got to get away.

Your blue Ford will be perfect. My daughter and I will be ready to escape soon. The bottle of will-sapping pills is almost empty. That monster brings my daughter Coke from the store, then he leaves us alone all evening. We must do something. Be ready!''

"I'm glad that you found a cat. The way he just walked in your window is a wonderful sign. Now maybe that mouse will stop bothering you. Pets are such a comfort. My son-in-law won't let us have one."

Next:

"You should get to bed earlier. It's not good for you to work all night. I like your new record too. Tell your girlfriend that she looks better now she has lost some weight. Make sure your car always has a full tank of gas. We must be ready at all times."

Weeks later came:

"Tonight's the night. *He* will be gone. Park your car five doors away— with the motor running. At exactly midnight step into the hall and cough three times. My daughter and I will meet you and make our escape. God bless you."

At the appointed hour I opened my door and coughed three times. Nothing happened. Five minutes later I tried again. Nothing!

I went back to work. A few days later, I passed the mother in the hall and tried to talk to her. Frantically she looked around and hurried off.

I moved away shortly afterward. I wonder how the next tenant fared.

Only in a Hitchcock movie is everything explained in the end.

THE CRITIC

"**H**EY, I got a job for you," said my friend Dan, "*The Oracle* needs a drama critic."

"What's *The Oracle*?" I asked.

The year was 1952. My wife Marjorie and I had just arrived on Cape Cod with our small son Scott.

"It's a local paper. You get it in the mail every week free. I've got a copy here."

I looked through its few tiny pages, which consisted of nothing but ads and one amusing cartoon. I chuckled.

"The cartoon is by Ed Smith. He's the editor/illustrator/distributor. He even folds it by hand. Until recently he and his family lived in an old abandoned house without heat, electricity, or . . ."

"I'll do it," I interrupted. "It sounds like the perfect publication for me."

A week later Marjorie and I prepared for my initiation into the world of journalism.

"You get the babysitter while I feed Scott," she said, "Of course, it doesn't prove much. He just keeps throwing up the formula."

"Maybe he's allergic to Cape Cod water," I suggested.

"Yes," sighed Marjorie, "I guess I'll have to try making it with Poland Spring water or something."

"Who's the babysitter this time?" I asked.

"A retired minister. He charges twenty-five cents an hour," she said.

"Inflation, inflation," I said, shaking my head as I left.

We went to the Orleans Arena Threatre box office.

"Seats are $1.50 apiece," announced the attractive young lady at the window.

"I'm the critic from *The Oracle*," I announced.

"The what?" said the young lady.

"*The Oracle*,"

"Oh, that little giveaway. Do they have a critic?"

"*Now* they do," I said.

The lights blinked.

"I'll let you work it out with the producer," she said hurrying away, "I'm starring in this damm thing."

"We can't give you any of the good seats," said the producer ducking through the bottom half of the door to the box office, "But we can stick . . . uh, put you in the balcony if you don't mind being all by yourselves."

The play was quite bad. It seemed to be about some teenagers in Australia. Only near the end of the piece did we learn that everyone was supposed to be middle-aged.

"They could at least have put some white gunk in their hair," I grumbled as we left.

"It's awfully hard to wash out," suggested Marjorie helpfully. "Anyway, just mention everyone by name."

"You may not be allowed back into the theater," said *Oracle* editor Smith later in the week. He showed me a letter from an angry lady. "I would cancel my subscription to your publication," it finished, "Except that we get it free whether we want it or not."

"Also *The Cape Codder* loved it," mused Ed.

"What's *The Cape Codder*?" I asked.

"That's our rival," he chuckled. "They actually charge a few cents for the paper. Our circulation is much bigger than theirs."

"Of course," I concluded, "Your circulation consists of everyone in town who receives mail."

A few weeks passed and the Compass Players (as they called themselves) at the Arena Theatre put on some excellent shows, which I was happy to note. Eventually they produced a flawed but effective version of Lorca's *Blood Wedding*. I praised their handling of this grim masterpiece.

"Your rival in *The Cape Codder* hated it," said Marjorie, "He intimated that it was dirty and said that he wouldn't want his sixteen-year-old baby sitter to see it. He felt that the Compass Players were 359 degrees off course."

"Must we lower the level of theatre on Cape Cod to the taste of sixteen-year-old babysitters," I thundered pompously in next week's *Oracle*, "Also, 359 degrees off course is pretty good steering."

"*The Oracle* has a new critic who seems to take himself too seriously," replied *The Cape Codder*, "Also he seems awfully influenced by Walcott Gibbs."

"*Walcott*! Who's this Walcott Gibbs?" I countered a week later, "Some relation to Jersey Joe?"

The storm in a chowder cup finally simmered down.

"Thank you," said the producer. "You said all the things we couldn't say. One actress is hurt, though. You said she was 'very nasty'."

"Actually, I said that she was brilliantly bitchy. Someone at the paper changed it."

"Yes," added Marjorie, "That was our retired-minister-babysitter. He's working at *The Oracle* now. He thinks 'bitchy' is a dirty word."

"Not as dirty as critic", said the producer.

LESSONS WITH MRS. LUCE

"**C**LARE Boothe Luce wants you to give her some lessons in egg tempera," said my agent.

The year was 1954. I was 28.

"Why did she pick *me*?" I asked.

"Well, actually she wanted Paul Cadmus, but he doesn't want to do it."

"O.K. But isn't Mrs. Luce sick? Arsenic poisoning or something?"

"Yes. She was our ambassador, or ambassadress, to Italy. The white-lead paint on the ceiling of her bedroom flaked and sifted down while she was asleep . . ."

"Nobody in Italy believes a word of *that*," I said.

"Anyway," he continued, "She needs some therapy while she's recuperating. Egg tempera should be good therapy."

"Egg tempera drives most people *crazy*."

"Give it a try. Her secretary will call you. And be sure to wear a tie."

"While I paint?" I asked. "How much is she paying me?"

"Don't worry," said my agent.

Actually Mrs. Luce called me herself.

"What's your address?" she asked.

"Well, uh," I stalled, "My studio is pretty messy. And you'll have to walk through a hearing-aid office. Everything's covered with dust. And the white lead paint on the ceiling is flaking. Also . . ."

"I can come next Friday," she said firmly.

"I really think your place would be . . ."

"Friday at, let's say, 2:00," she finished.

"O.K.," I agreed.

I set to work with broom and mop, feeling like Hercules attacking the Augean Stables.

7

"A distinguished-looking woman is coming here for painting lessons,"
I announced to the owner of the hearing-aid office, "Just show her back to
my, uh, studio."

"Do you think she can stand the shock?" asked the owner, winking at
his assistant, "Those rotting eggs weave a powerful spell."

The assistant pantomined fainting while holding his nose.

Mrs. Luce arrived on the dot and looked around hesitatingly as she searched
for a civilized place to deposit her beautiful coat. I dusted off a rickety chair
for her and pulled out my unrefrigerated eggs. Luckily, the two I chose
were reasonably fresh. The lesson seemed to go well, and Mrs. Luce was
relaxed and cheerful. After a couple of hours, she decided the lesson was
over.

"Next time we'll do it at my place," she suggested, trying not to look
at the cobwebs. She gave me her address.

"Isn't that the building where Greta Garbo lives?" I asked.

"Mmm," she said, smiling thinly. "Come at 12:00. We'll have lunch."

She left regally, dusting herself off ever-so-slightly.

"Was *that* who I think it was?" asked the owner, bursting into my studio.

"Of course," I said nonchalantly as I sloshed my egg yolk.

"How did it go?" asked my agent later.

"Good," I said ungrammatically, "By the way, how much is she paying
me?"

"We'll work that out later," he said quickly, "The important thing is to
establish the contact. Maybe you can talk her into a portrait. Or get her
interested in a painting."

"I'm no good at that sort of thing."

"Something will come of this. Don't worry. And take a taxi to her place."

Next week at the appointed time I made my way up to Greta's apartment
house, weighed down with paint jars, eggs, panels, etc. I had a little trouble
with the doorman, who wanted to send me around to the service entrance,
but my beautiful new necktie finally persuaded him to allow me access to
Valhalla.

"Say hello to Miss Garbo," I called back, but he didn't seem to hear
me. I was greeted by Mrs. Luce's secretary.

"Clare is really looking forward to this," she said. "You seem to be
very good therapy for her. Go ahead and set up in the livingroom."

"What's for lunch?" I asked.

"Lambchops for you. Gerbers for her," she called back.

A few minutes later, as I munched my lambchop, Mrs. Luce began to

ask me questions about myself in the tradition of "drawing out" the shy
newcomer. She soon found out that I grew up in Nevada.

"I wrote a play about Nevada," she said.

"Which one was that?" I asked.

"*The Women*," she said.

"Only a little bit of it," I said, attacking my peas.

"So, you know my work?" she said, quite pleased.

"Yes, even what you call Globaloney."

"Ah, yes, Globaloney," she mused, toying with her puree of Gerber's
turnips. "Well, that was just a publicity stunt."

"I've never been sure what it meant," I said.

"I feel," she said, "that this whole idea of 'one world' is, well, 'Globaloney.' Each country is actually out for its own interests."

She looked wistfully at my vanishing potatoes and stirred her baby food
into abstract patterns. "Where did you go to college?"

"I'm a Yaleman," I said.

"Yes, a Yaleman," she purred! "Most men say they went to Harvard,
or Princeton, or whatever. But men who went to Yale always say rather
touchingly, 'I'm a Yaleman'."

"Actually," I said, tensing, "I was enrolled at Harvard, and the Navy
sent me to Wesleyan."

"Which of my other plays have you seen?" she asked quickly.

"Well, I haven't actually *seen* any," I replied. She looked hurt. "But
I've read them all and seen the movie versions."

"What's your favorite? Not counting the one about Nevada."

"I guess I like the one where the Nazi was poisoned, stabbed and shot
just after he had a heart attack."

"That Would be *Margin for Error*! One of my more melodramatic efforts
. . . but fun. Let's get to work," she said, daintily pushing away the swirls
of colored food.

We went once again through the ritual of separating the egg yolk from
the white. She looked hungrily at this latter as it took its viscous exit down
the drain.

"Show me how to paint grass," she said.

I pulled out my rusty razor blade and demonstrated.

"And now sky," she chortled.

I pulled out my sponges.

"And rocks," she called out gleefully.

I pulled out my various toothbrushes.

"Don't you ever use a paint brush?" she asked.

"Eventually," I said, flinging some paint onto the panel next to her beautiful upholstery.

Just then I could hear the front door open, and Henry Luce walked in. He was back from one of his numerous world voyages. Mrs. Luce flung herself into his arms and began to kiss him. Then they went into the hall to snuggle a little. It was touching and unexpected. Finally they came back, arm in arm, and she introduced me to the great man. He was shy and inarticulate. After looking around at the chaos, he mumbled something inaudible and hurried away.

"Now, let's paint hair," chuckled Mrs. Luce.

"Don't *you* want to try?" I asked.

"No, this is too much fun," she laughed excitedly, "Now . . . ice. How do you paint ice?"

Hours later I began to pack up. When Mrs. Luce was not looking, I tried to wipe some splattered paint from the arm of a chair.

"Can I keep these?" she asked, indicating the small paintings I had executed.

"I—guess so," I said as I headed for the hall.

"This is the best therapy she's had since she came back from Italy," whispered the secretary, "Her eyes are sparkling!"

"Let's do this again soon," said Mrs. Luce, coming back in.

"Actually, I'm leaving for Cape Cod in a couple of days," I said.

"For how long?" asked Mrs. Luce, suddenly serious.

"About four months," I said guiltily.

"No, no," pantomined the secretary over the great lady's shoulder.

"Then we can't have another lesson next week?" queried Mrs. Luce.

"We can have lots more fun in the fall," I offered.

"Give up your summer!" pantomined the secretary desperately.

"I'll call you in September," I said, edging toward the door.

"You *do* that," said Mrs. Luce.

I told my agent about all this. He sighed gloomily.

"You know, summer in New York isn't as bad as most people think," he mused, eyeing me carefully.

"*No*," I said. "The kids would never forgive me. And I don't even know if I'm getting paid."

"Something will . . . Oh, go ahead," he said sadly, "After all, you can now say that you have two paintings in the Luce collection."

When my family and I returned in September, I phoned the Luce apartment. I was told that Mrs. Luce was not available. The secretary said that she would contact me if she could find the time. She didn't call.

Several years later I was commissioned to paint my first *Time* cover.

"See," said my agent, "I told you that something would come of it."

"No," said the Timeditor, "She had nothing to do with it. I saw your work at the Whitney Annual."

About the payment. I'm still waiting.

1957—MY FIRST *TIME* COVER

" "Is this Robert Vickrey?'' asked the voice on the phone.

"Yes," I said, "Who's this?"

"I'm an editor at *Time* magazine," said the voice.

"Fred, is that you? C'mon. Who is this really?"

"No, I *am* a *Time* editor," said the voice.

"Excuse me," I said, "I have a practical joker friend who . . ."

"O.K. O.K.," said the voice, "I saw your work at the Whitney Annual. Can you come and see me tomorrow at one o'clock?"

"Sure," I said, "I'll be there."

I told Marjorie about it.

"Be sure and wear a tie," was all she said.

"Would you be interested in painting Christian Dior for a cover?'' asked the Timeditor the following day.

He showed me several photographs.

"He looks like Alfred Hitchcock," I said, adding quickly, "One of my favorite faces."

"We need it in about three weeks," he said, "Can you do it?"

"I'll try. I work in egg tempera. It's a slow process."

"Will it be dry?" he asked.

"Oh, yes. It dries in a few seconds."

I took the material to my studio (in back of the hearing-aid office) and started to work, putting aside a painting of a St. Vincent nun, her beautiful winged cornette floating about her face.

The longer I worked on the portrait, the more my subject looked like Hitchcock. I decided to show him holding a huge pair of shears that looked faintly menacing. The viewer could not be sure whether he was about to attack a bolt of cloth or a model. I called *Time* to discuss my idea.

"Dior never touches shears or scissors or anything like that," said the editor, "But if you think it will make a good cover, go ahead and do it. We'll send you an assortment of instruments."

"I need a hand to hold the shears."

"That's your problem," said the voice.

"Would you like your hand to be on the cover of *Time*?" I asked the owner of the hearing-aid store.

"What?" he asked, cupping his ear comically and winking at his assistant.

"No, really, I mean it, "I said.

"O.K.," he said, chuckling, "Which one do you want? I charge less for the left one."

He sobered up a little when I showed him the assortment of lethal objects.

"I'll have to fatten up your knuckles," I said, stirring my egg yolk.

"Why don't you use fresher eggs?" he said, turning away.

"I don't have a refrigerator here," I said.

"What do you expect for $50 a month, including electricity?" he said in a friendly way.

"How's the great *Time* cover hand?" asked his assistant playfully, peeking in the door.

The cover appeared a few weeks later. I rushed out early on Monday morning and bought a copy. It wasn't as good as I wanted it to be, but I was walking on air. I went from one newsstand to another just to look at it nestling among all the other great magazines. I bought several copies, all in different places. I wanted to compare the quality of the reproductions, I rationalized.

When I returned to the hearing-aid office, everyone was very quiet. A copy of the magazine lay on the desk.

"I thought you were kidding," said the owner. He held up his hand. "You didn't get my thumb right."

"We artists change everything," I said mysteriously, as I went into my studio and pulled out the nun painting I had been working on.

A few years passed. In a movie this would be symbolized by pages flying off a calendar. Christian Dior died. But the St. Vincent habit seemed eternal, having survived the centuries. In the early 60's, however, the winds of change swept through the Church, and the beautiful cornettes were replaced by new, more efficient tailoring. The original headresses were designed for clean air and bicycles. They could not survive in our polluted atmosphere, and they wouldn't fit into cars. The habits, once blessed, must not be allowed to fall into unconsecrated hands. So all were burned.

The Saint Vincent Order is an order of poverty. For centuries the nuns have begged with their small bowls. Ironically, the new, more sensible habits were designed by—the Christian Dior studio. Without charge, I assume.

As I turned once more to paint my favorite subjects (the way I remember them) I consoled myself with the thought that all over the world these nuns were begging. . . . .wearing Christian Dior originals!

GOLDEN DAYS

Most young parents are very relaxed about childcare these days. The safety pin and diaper are no longer forbidden mysteries to fathers. Even the warmed-up bottle now holds no fears. Things were different years ago. When Marjorie and I were young, our maneuvers seemed to achieve the complexity of a Rube Goldberg machine.

We used to live in a ground-floor apartment in New York City, quite near the Bowery whose inhabitants sometimes slept on our doorstep. The building superintendant, whom we'll call Adolph, would expel them from the premises with a swift kick that looked suspiciously like a goose step. He would also spike the tires of our friends' cars when they parked too near his sacred portals. And he often purloined our cream and butter from the back hall in the early morning.

In those days I painted from noon til 2:00 a.m., except for time out to play with the children. I worked in a corner of the livingroom, surrounded by a collapsible fence to ward off the depredations of our three-year-old son Scott. A typical evening went like this.

"I'm tired," said Marjorie, "I think I'll turn in. Can you look in on Kiki? Remember, she cries every night from 12:00 to 1:00 for no reason. Give her a cuddle, even though it won't do much good."

"Sure," I said, adjusting the visor on my fisherman's cap, which was designed to keep the light from the 200-watt bulb from shining into my eyes.

"Scott is down for the night," said Marjorie, "But he'll be up at 6:00 or 7:00."

"Don't worry," I said, "I'll just listen to Long John Nebel on the radio. He's on from midnight till 5:00."

"Who's he having tonight?" asked Marjorie dubiously.

"A man who claims to have been captured by Martians. He's bringing a pancake they gave him."

"Why didn't he eat it?"

"If he'd eaten it, he couldn't have been on Long John's show," I said impatiently.

"Does this man get *paid* for being on the show?"

"Of course not."

"Then what's the use of it all?"

"You don't understand. All space nuts want to be on Long John's show. It's like winning the Academy Award. Nobody gets paid for being on *that*."

"I'm going to bed," said Marjorie, shaking her head. "By the way, don't forget to pull in the milk and butter before Adolph steals it."

"Have a happy," I said, stirring up some more egg yolk.

I painted for an hour or so, and then Kiki let me know that she was unhappy. I calmed her down till she went back to sleep on schedule.

"I've had your pancake analyzed," said Long John, "It seems to have been made with *Aunt Jemima* mix."

"Me and the Missus just brought you what we got. It ain't our fault if the Martians have the same formula," said the guest testily.

At 2:00 I began to get sleepy.

"It's all a Martian plot to flouridate our water and destroy our Precious Bodily Fluids," continued the guest.

"With *Aunt Jemima?*" asked Long John, losing patience.

"I've got to get to bed," I said groggily, "Enough is enough."

I heated up Kiki's bottle, put it in a thermos bag, and hung it on the outside doorknob of her room. Then I pulled a mattress out of the nearby closet and put it on the floor. I checked Scott and Marjorie to see if they were O.K, giving each a little kiss.

"There ain't no reason why they can't have *Aunt Jemima* on Mars," droned our friend from the radio, which I put next to my head on the floor as I fell asleep. I didn't want to miss a bit of this.

Sure enough, at 5:00, Kiki began to cry. Half awake, I reached up mechanically, took the still-warm bottle out of its thermos bag and handed it to her. She was waiting in her crib just inside the door, as called for by the ritual. She grabbed it and fell back, gurgling happily. The radio droned on, "Maybe the Martians invented this *Aunt Jemima* stuff and passed the formula on to we Earthlings."

Marjorie groaned in her sleep. Scott whimpered slightly. A distant clock struck. I heard the clinking of the milkman's bottles. Remember, I was sleeping just inside the back door.

"Ah, it must be the milkman from Mars," I mumbled, "He's delivering our *Aunt Jemima* pancake batter."

His footsteps faded. I heard a quiet voice humming the *Horst Wessel Song*.

I have three seconds before Adolph strikes, my fuddled mind thought.

Still flat on my back, I reached up to the knob, opened the back door, and scooped in the dairy products.

"Schweinhundt," I heard (or thought I heard) from the shadows.

I chuckled maliciously as I passed once more into the arms of Morpheus. The night was over. I slept the sleep of the just.

Marjorie arose at 7:00 to feed and take care of Scott. Then she stepped over me, took Kiki out of her crib, and carried her to the front room. This was my signal to get up, fall into the living-room hide-a-bed and resume my fitful slumber. Marjorie then gathered up the dairy products and put them in the refrigerator. At 11:00 she awakened me with a cup of coffee. We lived at the bottom of an airshaft and no light ever filtered into our bedroom/living-room.

"It's still night!" I moaned.

"No, it's just a cloudy day," she said, "What would you like for breakfast?"

"*Aunt Jemima* pancakes," I muttered, shakily.

"You'll have to have them without butter," she said, "Adolph was too fast for you."

MACY'S PARADE

On Thanksgiving we all like to sit comfortably in front of television and watch the Macy's parade. Many years ago some of us enjoyed this great event in a different way.

"Scott wants to see the Macy's parade," said Marjorie.

"Is he old enough?" I asked.

"Three and a half is old enough,"

"I could take him to a bar. We could watch it on TV."

"We *could* get our own set,"

"I've never seen anything that would justify such a drastic move,"

"All our friends have one," she sighed, wistfully.

"Maybe next year," I grumbled.

On the following morning Scott and I took the subway to upper Central Park West, where the parade was grouping. I figured that we could watch the marchers getting ready. Unfortunately a large portion of New York City had the same idea. The crowd was six deep. I hoisted young Scott onto my shoulders.

"What's going on?" I asked.

"Dunno, Daddy," he called down. "I see a big mouse!"

"That's Mighty Mouse," I said. "He's been around for years."

"And lots of other big animals," called Scott.

"What do they look like?" I asked, as my shoulders began to ache.

"Big doggie," said Scott, as I studied the tailoring on the overcoat shoulders around us.

"Soldiers, Daddy," said Scott.

"That's the band," I said, shifting his weight from my left to my right shoulder. "When did you get so heavy?"

18

"Balloons. Clowns and balloons. I want a *balloon*." he shouted.

"I'll buy you one if you can reach it," I said, studying the corkscrew curls of the woman ahead of me.

"Parade's starting, Daddy," chortled Scott.

"I can tell from the music," I moaned. "The band sounds great."

"Ice cream," pleaded Scott. "I'm hungry."

"Call to the ice cream man," I said shifting his weight back to my left shoulder.

"Don't pass it over me," said the lady with the corkscrew curls.

"Or me," said the man in front of *her*.

"I'll get you one later," I called to Scott above the sound of the music.

"Ooh," moaned the crowd at the passing wonders.

"What's happening?" I asked.

"Big dog," called Scott gleefully.

"Yes, I can see the tip of one ear."

I studied the intricate bandana pattern of the mother on my left, as a roar of approval went up from the crowd.

"Good, good," called out Scott.

"Amazing," said a very tall man, blocking my view.

"Why is it so quiet all of a sudden?" I asked.

"Parade's gone," said Scott sadly, "Didn't you love it, Daddy?"

"Best parade I ever heard," I muttered, as I lowered him from my aching shoulders.

"More, Daddy, more. Can we see it again? Can we?"

"Actually, we *can*. We could catch the subway down to 34th Street and see it all over again."

"Let's go," said Scott.

We took the crowded Downtown Local, standing all the way.

"Don't let go of Daddy's hand," I cautioned, as the doors opened and closed.

"MEET MISS SUBWAY," I read in an overhead poster." Pert, Vivacious Ginger Johnson. Hobby: Taxidermy." The doors opened at 42nd Street. "Ginger's ambition—" the doors began to close—"to find the perfect milkshake." Scott yanked loose and ran out. Frozen with horror, I rushed to the door and began to beat on the glass, through which I saw him careen into the arms of a maternal-looking woman. I smashed out all the glass with my hands.

"Hold on to him," I yelled as the train began to move. "I'll take the next one back."

Someone more clear-headed than I pulled the safety cord, the subway stopped, and—miracle of miracles—the door opened and I retrieved Scott.

Later, a kindly employee bandaged my hands and asked if I wanted to go to a hospital.

"No," I said. "We have an important engagement. Can I pay for the broken window?"

"No charge," he said with a smile.

Scott and I hurried down to 34th Steet and saw the parade again. Or at least *he* did. On the way home I said to him, "Remember now, don't tell Mommy about this. She'll just worry."

"Okay, Daddy," said Scott. "What about the bandages?"

"We'll think of something to tell her," I groaned, massaging my shoulders with my bandaged right hand. My left hand gripped Scott ferociously.

"Remember, now," I whispered as we entered our apartment.

"How did it go?" asked Marjorie as she burped our baby daughter.

"Mmm, fun," I said.

"Daddy smashed up his hand and stopped the train. I got lost. We saw the parade twice. Can we do it again next year?"

"You guys win," I said! "We'll get TV."

BURGLARS I HAVE KNOWN

I HAVEN'T known too many burglars personally, but there have been a few to whom I felt akin. According to Parkinson's Second Law (I think) each businessman progresses until he reaches the level of his incompetence. Here are some burglars who have evidently reached such a level.

Although Majorie and I have owned our home in Orleans for many years, we used to live in Connecticut during the school season so that our children could be with their friends. We would leave our Orleans house heated just enough so that the pipes would not burst. One winter we drove up and found that we were the victims of that most subtle form of crime—space burglary. Nothing was stolen, but somebody was living in our house when we weren't there. Victor Moore did that in the film *It Happened On Fifth Avenue.*

Anyway, we arrived and found our house lighted up. The space burglars evidently heard us come in the front door, and they bolted out the back. However, they left the table set and dinner cooking on the stove! We were tired, and it was late—so we ate the dinner. It was quite good.

A friend tells of some characters he met who deserve some sort of Burglar's Booby Prize. His house in New Hampshire was robbed in the winter when snow was on the ground. He came back unexpectedly, appraised the situation, and called the police. The culprits had stolen the television and several frozen steaks. He and the local police (no doubt using the latest in modern technology) simply followed the footsteps to the burglars' house and caught them red-handed—or red-lipped, since they were eating the steaks. Everything else was intact. Not much could be done about the steaks, though.

I personally came face to face with the world's most incompetent burglar in New York City many years ago. Marjorie and I lived in a ground floor apartment on Washington Square with our small children. My so-called studio, where I painted huge, incomprehensible allegories, was next to the kitchen where the radio was located. By turning it up, I could hear my favorite classical music on WNYC while I worked.

The children were at nursery school. Marjorie was at her desk saving the world from fascism. Suddenly I heard the radio in the kitchen change stations from Beethoven to Cugat. I continued to paint for a minute or two before my mind (such as it is) began to function. In that pre-computer world, radios did *not* change stations by themselves. I carefully rinsed the egg tempera off my brush and went into the kitchen, where I found a small man on his hands and knees wiping the floor. I also noticed that a can of bacon grease on the window sill had been knocked over. No *sensible* burglar would stop to clean up his mess and choose his theme music *so* carefully. Also the fact that the radio was on would have alerted him that we were home.

"What are you doing here?" I asked.

He stood up looking much like the wonderful Mexican clown, Cantinflas.

"No speak," he said, tapping his lips.

With the glibness of Wilde, I asked, "What do you want?"

He fished out some coins which he offered me and asked with an innocent smile, "You sell cigarettes here?"

The profit margin was not enticing enough, and fearing what he might do next, I pointed to the entryway and said, "There's the door. Would you like to use it?"

"Si, senor," he replied with a little salute and disappeared at something resembling the speed of light.

When I told the superintendent about all this, he was furious. He felt that I should have wrestled this Napoleon of Crime to the ground while Marjorie called the police. As I was being chastised by him for my delinquency, his wife, who was sitting by their window, piped up, "Was he a little dark-haired man with a cap and a mustache?" I replied in the affirmative.

"Oh, yes," she said, "I've been watching him all day. He's been going up and down the fire escapes—going into all the apartments. He had a very sweet face."

However, the most insulting burglar robbed me at a New York tennis club a few years later. While I was playing, he broke into my locker where I had stored a small painting and a Timex watch.

He stole the watch.

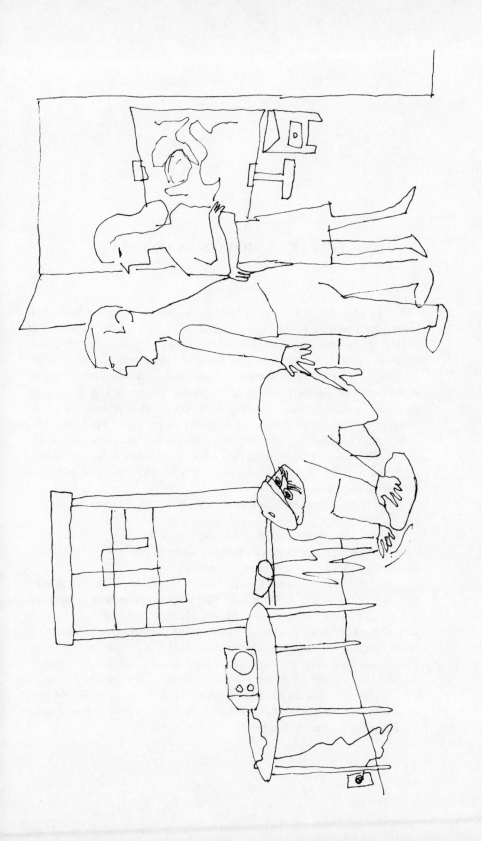

THIRTEEN MOVIES IN ONE DAY

W HEN Marjorie and I lived in New York City we were members of an organization called Cinema-16, a group of cinemaddicts who would stop at nothing in a wild attempt to see every rare film ever made. This obsession came to a head when we were told Eastman House in Rochester was organizing a weekend of seldom-seen masterpieces. These films could be viewed only on the premises of the museum, since many of them were illegal or "pirated" prints. As long as they were shown under these circumstances (without admission) no disputing owner could interfere.

At first it looked as if Marjorie and I would not be able to go on this happy holiday because we couldn't get a babysitter. Then, at the last minute, we found a hardy (perhaps foolhardy) soul who was willing to undertake this Herculean labor.

"Have a good weekend," she said as we left. "By the way, what's this trip for?"

"We're going to the movies." we said.

Amos Vogel, the founder of Cinema-16 met us and gave us the details of what lay ahead. We started on our odyssey.

About 35 of us left Grand Central Station at six o'clock on Friday after the close of the normal working day. There was no thought of plane travel in 1957. This delightful trip took almost eight hours. Marjorie and I carried several books with us, but we had not foreseen the following handicap: the lights on the train constantly went on and off. I don't mean they flickered. *That* would have been too easy. The timing (by our watches) was approximately four minutes *off* to one minute *on*. Fine for Dos Passos's "camera eye" techniques, but no good for Tolstoy, which I had in hand. We tried to snooze, but the sudden blaze of light would wake us every time. Finally we arrived at Rochester and hastened to our motel.

24

"I've left a six o'clock call for all of us," said Vogel cheerfully. "We have to eat and be at the auditorium by eight o'clock." It was three before we got to sleep.

Our heavy-lidded band arrived at its destination the next morning. We stopped to admire some of the fascinating exhibitions.

"No time for that," said Vogel sternly, as he pulled us away from the ancient projectors and battered cameras. Like a Judas goat he led us into the theater where we were given a program describing the 12 films we were to see that day. Many local aficionados had joined us by this time.

First on the agenda were several little-known Garbo pieces, like *As You Desire Me* and *Romance*. The latter, by the way, contains my favorite Garbo lines:

"Ven I was young, we were very poor. But we had lots of friends—all of them mices."

Next we watched Lana Turner's debut in *They Won't Forget*. She was 16 as she walked down a peaceful village street in her soon-to-be notorious sweater. Five minutes later she was murdered.

Von Sternberg's *Docks of New York* came on. "This doesn't look like my type of film," said Marjorie. "I think I'll take a nap."

Later, lunch was brought in to us in cardboard boxes. "We're going to continue while you're eating," announced Vogel from the stage. "And a bit of good news. A rare Japanese film has been scheduled by mistake for this afternoon. It *must* be shown today because it has already been advertised in the paper." A few moans were heard through the ham sandwiches and apples.

"Spell me," I said to Marjorie after the first few minutes of this murky masterpiece.

"Okay," she said, "I'll nap during the Chaplin things. He's such an unpleasant little man."

She woke me an hour later.

"How did the film come out?" I asked.

"The whole cast committed suicide," she replied.

While Marjorie slept, I greatly enjoyed the two Chaplin offerings, *Shoulder Arms* and *The Pilgrim*, which ran about 30 minutes each. Remember, most of these movies lasted an hour and a half or less. The double feature of the '30s necessitated this time limit.

Dinner At Eight came on approximately at dinnertime. Here is my favorite exchange from this opus.

Jean Harlow: In the world of the future they say that everything will be done by machines.

Marie Dressler (looking her up and down): My dear, that's something *you'll* never have to worry about.

In the next film, *Grand Hotel*, one of the characters came out with "I'm tired and my eyes hurt." The whole audience burst into laughter and applause.

"I'm going out for a smoke," said Marjorie.

"Don't stay too long," I said. "There's something good coming up next."

"What's that?"

"Another Garbo."

She hurried up the aisle.

By midnight some of our group had left. "Shame, shame," hissed someone. Sleepy heads began to fall sideways all around us.

"Please stay," pleaded our fearless leader. "We have a really rare item coming up." He looked at his watch. "In about two hours."

"Way to go, Amos." shouted someone hoarsely.

In the flickering light we saw a few more deserters skulking out. "Dilettantes," I murmured. More tempers began to fray.

"If I fall asleep," whispered the man next to me, "nudge me if there's something *really* good."

Our tastes may not be the same," I snapped.

"I wonder how the children are," mused Marjorie wistfully.

"First things come first," I growled.

We few, we happy few, we band of brothers (and sisters) cheered shakily as Vogel announced that the final surprise offering was . . . a dirty *Baron Munchhausen*. Hitler's film unit was shooting this when the Allies overtook them. Thus its legal ownership was in dispute. For some reason all of the Baron's female servants were stripped to the waist as they waited on him. This was supposed to improve Nazi morale. It didn't do much for ours. Several more souls left before the end of the segment. At 3:30 those of us who were left staggered back to our motel, which was 15 minutes away and fell into bed.

"What was it that Amos said at the end?" I asked Marjorie.

"We all have to be at the auditorium at eight o'clock tomorrow morning," she answered. "They've got three more for us before the train leaves at one o'clock."

PAINTING THE PRINCESS

W OULD you like to paint an Arabian Nights Princess?'' asked the Voice from *Time*. She's absolutely gorgeous—and 24 years old.''

"Why not?'' I replied.

"Everything's all set,'' said the voice a few days later. "She's willing to pose. Remember, she's never worn the veil. We're doing an article on —well, Women's Lib in Arabia. She's only 29 and very beautiful.''

"Last time you said she was 24.''

"No, no, 29. But first you'll have to have a physical. Company policy, We'll pay for everything, of course. How's your passport?''

"It lapsed,''

"Don't worry,'' sighed the voice, "We'll get you your physical *and* your passport. Can you leave in three days?''

I had my physical—and several shots. I went to pick up my passport at *Time*. While waiting I browsed through their latest edition. "Princess Aisha (34) is the symbol of the liberated Arabian woman,'' read the article. Time *really* marches on, I thought. "You look a little funny,'' said the editor.

"It's those typhoid shots. The doctor said they might give me some of the symptoms.''

"How about some Scotch?'' he asked opening another drawer. "Can you make it to the airport?''

"I'll give it my best shot,'' I said.

"Forget the puns, and remember, you have to change planes in Paris before you fly on to Rabat. I hope those shots wear off before you begin to paint,'' he said pointedly.

I reeled onto the plane and fell into a typhoidal sleep. Many hours later the stewardess shook me. "You have eight minutes to get through French customs and onto the next plane. We'll rush your luggage through. I'm

afraid you'll have to run all the way.'' The porter, my luggage, and I dashed
away frantically.

"Monsieur," called a little man in a beret clutching at my sleeve and
holding out some documents. "No dirty pictures now," I said, trying to
pull loose. We ran in tandem. My luggage and I were detained momentarily
by the customs inspector. "Monsieur, Monsieur," croaked my comrade
once more. "You have one minute," said the gate attendant. The little man
physically blocked my way and held up a note. "Don't take the plane," it
read. "The princess is here in Paris."

He then drove me to a small battered hotel. "We really have no room,"
said the desk clerk, "But *Time* says we *must* put you up. Every place in
town is taken. The automobile show is on."

"Ah, French culture," I mused.

"We do *not* guarantee hot water in that particular room," he said icily.

I checked in at *Time* headquarters. "The princess can't see you today.
Just call us every morning about ten o'clock," said the bureau chief. "If
she's in the mood, we'll work something out. Otherwise, you have the rest
of the day free—on an expense account," he added wistfully.

"By the way, how old is the princess?" I asked.

"About 38, I guess," he said.

For the next week she was *not* in the mood to pose. This left me with
the heavy burden of seeing every movie in Paris, remembering to tip the
usherette each time.

Finally a frantic phone call came, "Quick, she's just left for Morocco.
You and Bill McHale should get right down there."

"But Monsieur, the automobile show is over. Now you can have any
room you want," said the hotel clerk.

"How about hot water?" I asked. He gave a Gallic shrug.

Bill and I boarded the plane to Rabat. "I spend so much time on planes,"
mused Bill. "Statistics say I'll die on one."

"Let's have another gin and tonic," I suggested, toasting the recession
of my typhoid symptoms.

After a bumpy taxi ride, we settled into our hotel in the French Quarter.
"We just check in every morning," said Bill. "When the Princess is willing,
they'll tell us."

"Here we go again," I sighed, "By the way, how old is she?"

"Fortyish, I guess," said Bill.

We spent the next few days touring the Casbah and going to English
movies dubbed into French. *Richard III* was my favorite.

"She'll pose," said Bill on the fourth day. He rushed off to make final arrangements. I had my panel and my paint ready. All I needed was an egg. I called room service, "Two eggs—uh, deux oeufs—um, not cooked." "Oui, Monsieur," said room service.

Shortly afterward, two soft-boiled eggs arrived. "No," I called down, "Not cooked, pas cooked." Two more *very* soft-boiled eggs came. I called a third time. "We close now," said room service.

Bill arrived to announce that the limousine to the palace was waiting.

"Quick, where's the nearest grocery store?" I asked.

"They're all closed. Everything here closes in the middle of the day. But, wait, the *bar* stays open. They must have eggs for daiquiris and things."

We hurried down. A bartender who looked like Fernandel was on duty. Bill negotiated with him in French with much arm waving.

"What's going on?" I asked.

"He has eggs, but he's not allowed to sell us one."

"Tell him it's for the princess," I said.

More arm waving. Fernandel expressed Gallic disbelief.

"Tell him," I said, "it's to mix the paint with."

Fernandel made an obscene gesture of total derision. "Don't translate that one," I said.

"Your limousine is waiting," called the doorman.

Bill tried one more time. "Ahhh," said Fernandel, beaming with sudden understanding. With a little flourish he presented us with an egg.

"What did you tell him?" I asked in the limousine (a battered old Chevy).

"I told him you painted still lifes and wanted to paint a picture *of* an egg . . . not *with* an egg. *That* he was willing to believe."

The princess (like Queen Victoria) was not amused by our story or our lateness. As I settled down before her and the ladies of the court to paint, Bill photographed me at work.

"It's hot," I said. "May I remove my jacket?" "Oui, Monsieur," said Her Highness icily.

"Please sit still," I cautioned.

"One does not tell a princess what to do," whispered Bill.

I worked on wishing that she had not worn purplish-pink lipstick. Giggles came from behind me as I sketched in her nostrils. Tea full of mint was served in tiny glasses. I worked two more days awash in courtly cachinations and tannic acid. "Doesn't she have something more interesting to wear?" I asked. Servants brought me out dozens of dresses—all identical in style. "Could I look into her closet?" I asked. "Monsieur," said the shocked servant, "One does not—"

"Yes, yes, I know," I said.

I went looking for some interesting architecture for the background! "Just don't put in any graffiti," said Bill, "It may be obscene or revolutionary or something."

"It's time to hit the road," I said. We left for the airport in a beat-up Checkercab. Halfway there, it coasted to a stop. The driver muttered something, jumped out and began to hitchhike. "He's run out of gas," said Bill, "He'll get a couple of gallons and hitch a ride back."

"Why don't we take our bags and flag down another cab?" I asked.

"He's no dope. He's locked our luggage in the trunk," said Bill philosophically.

We actually made the plane and, in spite of Bill's gloomy predictions, we got safely home.

"Who's this 45 year old woman?" grumbled the editor at *Time*.

"That's what she looks like," I said.

The cover and story appeared shortly afterward with a brief article illustrated with Bill's photograph of me.

"What do you think?" I asked Marjorie.

"Well," she said, "You finally got your picture in *Time* and your *shirttail's* out."

LOOKING FOR PENNSYLVANIA STATION

A LONG, long time ago Pennsylvania Station was torn down. No one except the real estate brokers knew why. After all, it was one of New York City's great landmarks with its amazing metal and glass arches. For some strange reason, the outside was an imitation Greek temple.

Anyway, some committee decided to tear the whole thing down, carry the pieces out to Secaucus, New Jersey, and dump them in the marshes. *The New Yorker* published a great cartoon showing a truckful of rubble entering this swampy hamlet. The driver is asking a policeman, "Where shall I dump Penn Station?"

Eventually the new Madison Square Garden was constructed on this site, and the Penn Station trains continued to arrive and depart underground. We all missed those wonderful arches. Soon articles began to appear in the papers with photographs of broken columns and battered statues protruding from piles of New Jersey garbage.

What a great idea for a painting, I thought. A symbol of the contemporary art world. The Secaucus swamp, of course, symbolizing the critics. Perhaps some graffiti adorning these neo-classic remains could stand for the accepted art of our time.

Anyway, it was worth a visit.

Marjorie and I lived in Connecticut at this time with our four children. We were expected at her parents' place in East Orange for Sunday dinner.

"You mean all six of us plus the dog, the cat and the gerbil have to spend the day driving through the New Jersey swamps?" I queried.

"We'll leave the gerbil home," said Marjorie.

Then I got to thinking. We would have to go through Secaucus on the way . . . Maybe we could find Penn Station, and I might get some good ideas.

We set off in our overpacked station wagon. After some heated discussion we finally left the gerbil *and* the cat at home. We nailed the gerbil's cage to a beam in the middle of the play room ceiling.

"Let's see if the cat can outwit us this time," I said.

We allowed two hours for searching Secaucus, after which we would proceed to East Orange for dinner.

"How are we going to find Penn Station, Daddy?" asked my son Scott.

"We'll just look for the nearest policeman," I replied confidantly.

I took the many relevant newspaper clippings with me just in case.

In beautiful downtown Secaucus, we eased up to the first policeman.

"Stop holding your nose while I'm asking directions," I said to my four children. "The policeman may be insulted."

Little moans greeted my command.

"Could you please tell me where the remains of Penn Station have been deposited?" I asked in my most tactful voice.

He gave me a dirty look.

I repeated my question. He waved us on brusquely. After approaching two more policeman and failing to make communication, we gave up on the legal approach.

"Let's ask some bums," our daughter Nicole said. "*They* should know all about it."

This didn't work either. Time was passing.

"The Chamber of Commerce is probably closed on Sunday," said Marjorie.

"I don't think they'd tell us anyway," I said. "After all, this is not something they would be proud of."

We set off, newspaper clippings in hand, to search every dump in Secaucus.

"Why are we spending the whole day in these smelly places?" chanted the children.

"We're looking for Penn Station," I replied.

We knew from the photographs that there should be railroad tracks and telephone poles near the sought-after location. No one in Secaucus seemed to recognize these important landmarks. We approached a few more policemen—with no better results.

"Why are we doing this?" the children squealed once more.

Our dog Cocoa pantomined incontinence. Even *he* was anxious to get out of the garbage and back into the car. It's hard to hold your nose with a paw.

An hour later we were on the verge of something like the mutiny on the *Bounty*.

"Why? Why?" came the query.

"We're looking for Penn Station," I replied doggedly.

After getting stuck a couple of times, we spotted some telephone poles and railroad tracks.

"Ah, success at last," I called, as our wheels dug deeper into the garbage.

"We'll have to get the car washed tomorrow," said Marjorie.

"It may take a blow torch," said Scott.

"My nose is getting sore," said Carri.

"You're squeezing it too tightly," I said.

Cocoa moaned quietly in the corner next to Sean.

"It's too hot to roll the windows up and the stink is too awful if we roll them down," came a chorus.

"Be thankful you don't have to live here," I replied philosophically.

"East Orange, where I used to live, isn't *that* far away," mumbled Marjorie.

Well, we never did find Penn Station. Nobody in the area would admit that the community had been defiled by its stately ruins. Marjorie's parents were a bit miffed that we were two-and-a-half hours late for dinner.

We never did tell them why.

PAINTING KIM NOVAK

"WOULD you like to paint Kim Novak?" asked the Voice from *Time*.
"Sure," I said with all the cheek of 31 years.

"She's willing to pose for as long as you want in San Francisco. The cover story is about the movie, *Jeanne Eagels*, but she will actually be shooting *Pal Joey*."

As a great fan of John O'Hara's book, with its Chicago milieu, I was a little dubious about the transfer to San Francisco.

"Its closer to Los Angeles," said the voice from *Time*.

I asked if I could take my wife along.

"I guess so, as long as you both travel *coach*."

In those days (1957) the planes were propeller driven. The trip took 13 hours, and there was no food—at least in the coach section. However, we were allowed to get off in Chicago and purchase box lunches to eat in flight.

Marjorie and I arrived in LA as planned, and we were treated royally by everyone. We spent two days there discussing why Miss Novak could not pose. Eventually the word came through that she was in San Francisco at the Mark Hopkins Hotel. We flew from LA to San Francisco on a "Champagne Flight." The passengers could have all the champagne they wanted, and each lady on the plane received a free orchid. Since there were only four people on the flight, Marjorie was offered all the orchids she could handle. She settled for five or six.

"Please take some more," they pleaded with us as we fled from the plane leaving a trail of flowers behind us.

We were met at the airport by my brother, who lived nearby. He chauffeured us to the Mark Hopkins in a battered pick-up truck which even the Joad family would have rejected. The doorman didn't know quite how to handle the situation. He pulled our battered luggage from the back of the

35

truck and haughtily called for a bellboy, as Marjorie and I passed into the lobby to register.

"Which way is north," I asked the startled clerk.

The stare he gave me conveyed decades of experience.

"You see, I need north light to paint by."

He summoned the manager.

"No one has ever asked that before," he said, whereupon I pulled out a compass (people think artists are unrealistic) and, pointing in the proper direction, said "I want a room on *that* side of the hotel."

He smiled thinly and assigned us our quarters.

The next day, Miss Novak was ready to pose. I wanted to look my best so (with Marjorie's permission) I had a topless shoe shine. This was a new craze limited to California at the time. The attractive young lady who worked on my pedal extremities was stripped to the waist. *Time*, of course, covered the expenses for this important touch of class.

Safe in the knowledge my shoes had never looked better, I waited in our luxurious suite for Miss Novak. She arrived clad in lavender slacks, lavender blouse, lavender neckerchief—and lavender hair. Yes, she had bleached her hair white and then added a slight lavender rinse. Her face was quite expressionless.

As the sittings progressed, she proved to be very likeable. Hours went by, and she began to describe her innermost thoughts—almost as if I were a psychiatrist. Her stream of consciousness went on and on. She told me of her singing and dancing lessons, her determination to master all forms of show biz. She wanted to be a really *great* actress, not just a sex symbol like Marilyn Monroe. She *almost* had an expression on her face when she made that statement. She was challenged by the competition with Rita Hayworth, one of her co-stars in *Pal Joey*.

"But she's fifteen years older than I am," she added.

Finally, in an attempt to get a more expressive portrait, I put a poster in the background showing her lying sexily on a tiger skin rug. She was chewing vigorously on a chain of pearls.

Suddenly she noticed that I was painting her with a three-quarter facial exposure. She had broken her nose many years before, and a tiny flaw was slightly visible from that angle. She stamped to the phone and called the studio. The moguls told her that they couldn't control the policies of *Time*. She became somewhat pacified when she saw that I wasn't including the tiny flaw in the portrait.

"You're leaving out the little flecks of ochre around my irises," she announced on the following day.

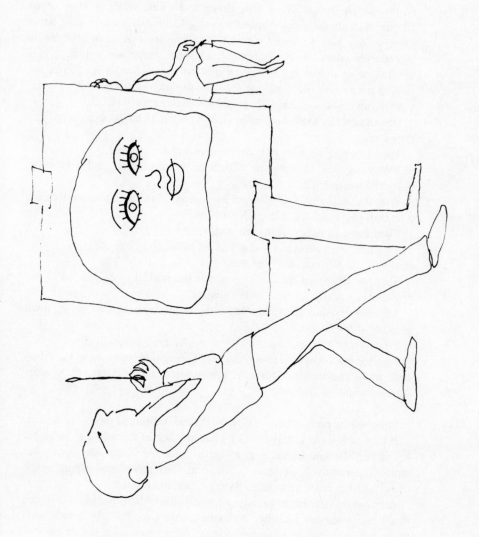

She was right.

"And my lashes are slightly longer."

She wore no makeup that I could see, except around the eyes. No lipstick, no powder, no rouge. Those little ochre flecks were *very* important. After all, she was almost single-handedly saving Columbia Studios from bankruptcy. They had her under contract for $750 per week—and refused to increase her salary. Harry Cohn, the head of the studio, was willing to give her the use of limousines and many other luxuries. *But no raise!* Her costars in most cases, were making four or five times as much. In her expressionless way, she was quite chagrined about these matters.

Desperately, I added some more violent posters in the background to jazz things up.

Then I started to block in her shoulders and neckerchief.

"Why are you painting me with a lavender kerchief and a lavender blouse?" she queried.

With the agility of Noel Coward I answered, "Because you are wearing a lavender kerchief and a lavender blouse."

"But I almost never wear such things,"

"You've worn them every day you've posed,"

"Well, its just not *me*," she fumed.

She then described the outfit in which she wished to be painted. I improvised it weeks later back in my studio.

The next day she called and told me the entire company was leaving town because of the "haze."

"You know how that ruins color photography," she said.

I replied that a slight haze is often very beautiful in such cases. She posed once more and then left for LA. I was peremptorily informed no more sittings would be allowed.

I finished the portrait back in New York, and it appeared shortly afterward.

It later turned out that Harry Cohn had engineered the whole affair to put her in her place, since she was trying to force the studio into paying her more. The extremely derogatory article in *Time* reproduced a photograph of her and her boss, captioned "Harry Cohn and Product."

A few years later I heard a radio interview in which my subject mentioned that I had made her look like an expressionless zombie. As James Bond said when he shot an assailant with a spear-fishing gun, "She got the point."

ON THE TRACK OF THE WORLD'S WORST MOVIE

LEPIDOPTERISTS constantly seek the world's rarest butterfly. Philatelists track down the single stamp where the ugly main image has been accidentally printed upside down. Gourmets search out the world's most rare and expensive food—Chinese snake urine—at $100 a spoonful. Why shouldn't a film buff spend an equal amount of time looking for the world's worst movie?

There are bad plays too. The world's worst may be *Time Out For Ginger*. This opus concerns a young girl who tries out for the boys' basketball team in high school—and makes it. This triumph, of course, destroys her stuffy parents' social life.

Certain ground rules must be observed in this quest for the Unholy Cinematic Grail. Films like the Bowery Boys' *Dig That Uranium, Abbot and Costello Meet Frankenstein*, or *Blondie Has Servant Trouble* don't count. No! They must be *big* stinkers—ambitious, expensive, and exquisitely rotten. The Medved Brothers have compiled *their* list of the worst films of all time, but I respectfully disagree with some of their choices. They have picked such movies as the low budget satire, *The Attack Of The Killer Tomatoes*, the kiddy hit, *Santa Claus Conquers The Martians*, and other such unworthy efforts.

In 1968 *The Legend Of Lylah Clare* seemed to be a likely entry in the sweepstakes. In most cases this movie closed before the customers could get to the theater. I had painted Kim Novak's portrait several years before and had been following her career ever since. Marjorie and I were determined to track down this turkey, but it came and went so fast that we couldn't catch it. Finally we noticed that it was playing at a drive-in theater quite far from where we lived in Fairfield, Connecticut.

"Don't count on its being there," said Marjorie. "Remember what happened the last few times."

I called the theater, long distance. A soothing mechanical voice assured me *The Legend of Lylah Clare* would be shown that night.

We rushed off, skipping dinner. We figured that we could eat at the drive-in snack bar. We got lost a few times, but we finally found our destination and approached, money in hand. All was dark. No one was in the box office. Only the inhuman beam of light shining on the screen gave hint that someone was in charge. Also there were two cars present, one obviously belonging to the projectionist-manager and the other to a solitary customer.

With money still in hand, I approached the darkened snack bar and banged loudly on the window. I felt there was no great hurry. After all, the second feature (shown first, of course) was still on. But Marjorie and I were getting hungry. Eventually a shadowy figure appeared.

"We're not open for food," he said. "But I can sell you some candy bars."

"I'll take about ten," I replied. "Are you going to show the Lylah Clare movie tonight?"

"As long as we have two cars."

It was becoming clear that if I admitted we were there without paying, the whole show would be cancelled. So, pocketing my New England morality (with my cash), I hurried back to our car.

"It's all right," I said to Marjorie, "as long as they have two cars, they'll show it."

I handed her a pile of candy bars and settled down to watch the end of the second feature.

It was a movie version of *Time Out For Ginger*. The studio had retitled it *Billie*. Patty Duke was starring, only now she was trying out for the *track team*. You see—NO BODY CONTACT. A real breakthrough! Two of the world's worst movies *on the same bill*.

"Don't be overconfidant," counseled Marjorie, gorged with chocolate, "They might still cancel the main feature."

Finally came the intermission. The snack bar was still dark, but the other car remained in place. We didn't look too closely at what the occupants were doing. Instead, we watched the projection booth nervously. The cartoons ended, and *The Legend of Lylah Clare* began. We were actually going to *see* it! My guilt at not paying was beginning to subside when another problem arose. *The other car drove away.* We two criminals were witnessing this great artistic event *alone*. We gobbled more candy bars while Kim

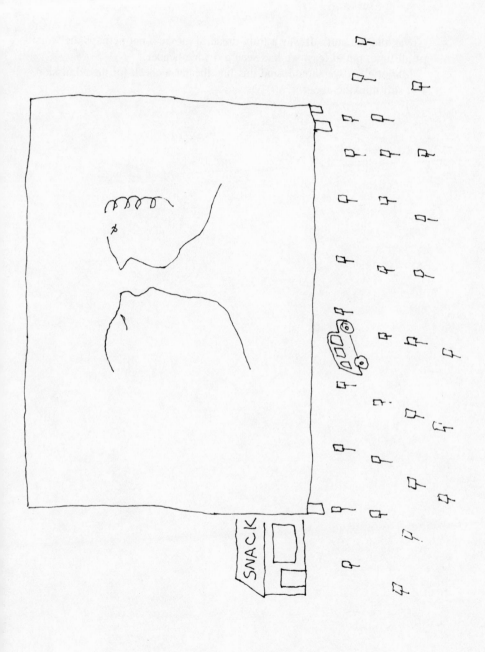

Novak did her stuff. It was a truly dreadful movie—not perhaps the worst of all time, but at least we had seen a double-header.

Marjorie felt we should send this fine theater a check for the admission. I'm still thinking about it.

TWELVE ANGRY JURYPERSONS

A FEW years ago I was called for jury duty. At first, I was miffed because it meant that I couldn't paint for two weeks. I expressed these thoughts to Marjorie.

"My God," she said. "It will be a good experience. You might help to right some terrible wrong, or save some innocent person's life."

"But I won't finish my painting. I'll miss my deadline."

"It'll be worth it," she said.

Then I got to thinking about all the great movie trials:

The Lady From Shanghai, where Everett Sloane, the defending attorney for Orson Welles is called as a hostile witness against his own client—and has to cross examine *himself* on the stand.

Twelve Angry Men, where the jurors battle and almost kill each other while arriving at a verdict.

Witness For The Prosecution, where Charles Laughton, fat, manipulative, and brilliant, outwits everyone and carries all before him.

The French movie, *Justice Is Done*, where every juror votes according to his own problems and prejudices.

"Yes, by George, I'll do it," I said to myself.

"Remember, you can't discuss it with me til it's over," said Marjorie.

I arrived dutifully at the court house and checked in. Being forewarned, I brought several books to read: Kafka's, *The Trial*, Dostoevsky's, *The Brothers Karamazov*, and Daisy Ashford's, *The Young Visitors*.

I sat there for a week, and they never called my name. I got a lot of reading done. Eventually I went up to the desk and asked how long this might go on. "If you're not called within six days, you can ask for a dismissal," I was told.

43

Oh well, I painted over the weekend and went to my legal reading room on the following Monday. On the afternoon of the sixth day (remember, that was the day God created man) I applied for dismissal. "One more hour and you can go free," the man said. That's when they called my name.

As prospective jurors, we were first questioned by the two lawyers. The prosecuting attorney looked just like Charles Laughton, and the defense attorney looked just like Everett Sloane. I figured that when I mentioned that I was an artist, I would be dismissed. However, this was the second trial of the case (the first jury was hung—*their* phraseology), and both lawyers were determined to get the whole thing over with. So they accepted me.

Anyway, the jury was eventually chosen: ten men and two women. We went to work, only now we came an hour later and left two hours earlier. The mills of justice grind slowly—and about three hours less per day.

In our jury box, we were arranged in alphabetical order. The woman on my left looked just like Josephine Hull. The man on my right looked just like Archie Bunker.

"Uh oh," said Archie. "Here comes the Judge." We all rose. This impressive figure looked like Minor Watson.

The basic case was as follows: A widow had been defrauded by a broker who subsequently died. She was suing the man she thought to be his partner for redress. And he was our friend Everett Sloane, who was defending himself.

Charles Laughton called, as his first witness—Everett Sloane, his opposing attorney. "He'll have to cross examine himself," I whispered to Archie. "Na, na," he whispered back. "That only happens in the movies."

"Now, Mr. Sloane, why did you do such and such?" thundered Charles Laughton to his diminutive opponent. Sloane answered all questions carefully and somewhat evasively. He knew his time would come.

At the end of this duel, Judge Watson said, "Mr. Sloane will now cross examine himself." Archie gasped.

"Now, Mr. Sloane, did you do such and such?" asked our defendant.

"I certainly remember no such transaction," he replied after some thought. And later, "Why, no. We were never partners, just friends."

"Now, Mr. Sloane, you mean to tell me that you sat in on all of these transactions with Mrs. Natwick just to be friendly," he thundered to himself.

"Why, yes," he said innocently, "That's all."

"Alright, alright," said Judge Watson finally. "Let's get on with it."

Charles Laughton tried to introduce some letters that would prove a business connection between the dead man and Mr. Sloane. Judge Watson would not admit them.

"Judge, this case is being carried on prejudicially," shouted Mr. Laughton.

"My actions are reviewable," said Judge Watson acidly. "Also don't call me Judge. I should be addressed as 'Your Honor' ".

"O.K., Judge," sneered Mr. Laughton, who then in desperation, called the defrauded widow to the stand.

"You notice she's worn the same dress for four days," said Josephine Hull.

"You are an evil man, Mr. Sloane," shouted our weeping widow, pointing accusingly at him. "Cheating a helpless woman."

"That's a very expensive bracelet she's wearing," said Josephine Hull.

"It's the old switcheroo," said Archie. "Now you see it, now you don't."

"The jury will disregard the witness's last outburst," said Judge Watson, knowing that we would not.

Finally the judge charged us, making it quite clear where his sympathies lay. We went to our jury room which looked just as awful as the set in *Twelve Angry Men.*

"I realize that I've been chosen alphabetically," said our foreman. (E. G. Marshall.) "But I *am* in charge," he said, eyeing us hostilely. "Now I don't want this to influence you, but I've just recovered from a cancer operation. So let's not string this out too long. First of all, who has to go to the john?" Three men filed out. "You ladies have much better equipment than us," commented E. G. Marshall to the two female jurors.

Finally, we set to work. "Does anyone have an idea how to start this thing?" asked E. G. Marshall. Nobody said a word. In my thin voice, I piped up, "I think he's guilty, but I don't think they've got the goods on him." Josephine Hull leaned over and whispered to me, "You remind me of my son. You both have the same sweet smile."

"The defendant has beady eyes like my brother-in-law," said one juror. "Shut up," said our foreman. "My doctor says I can't stand tension."

"My son wouldn't like this man," said Josephine Hull. I wondered which man she meant. The toilet flushed a few more times. Deliberation is a delicate process.

We did not come to blows like the jury in *Twelve Angry Men*, but we *did* finally arrive at a verdict. Remember, this was a civil (not a criminal) suit, and ten out of twelve votes were required for acquittal, which is what we had.

"Let's make it unanimous," said our foreman. "It will make us all feel much better."

"Fat chance!" said Archie.

"Never," said Josephine Hull.

"I'm thinking of changing my vote," I muttered.

"I think my son would have voted like you," said Josephine Hull.

"So the crook got off," said Archie.

"You voted for acquittal," I reminded him.

After the verdict, the judge thanked us all for doing an excellent job. He positively *beamed* his approval. Charles Laughton asked that we be polled in place, so that he could look each of his enemies in the eye. The wealthy widow (in the same dress) cried some more.

As we left the building, Josephine Hull gave me a little kiss on the cheek and once again told me that I reminded her of her son. We all parted, feeling uneasily that an unconvicted culprit had been loosed upon the world.

Six months later I received a check for my labors. It was for the sum of $16.83.

MUGGING, MURDER AND MUNITIONS

Our apartment in New York was just off Fifth Avenue. The block was lined with attractive trees. There was a church on one side of our building and another one across the street. A kindergarten was right next door.

We even had a lovably eccentric neighbor lady to provide us with entertainment. She was a dedicated snoop. Evidently she waited all day just inside the entrance to her apartment. Whenever she heard a noise in the hall, she would open her door, place an empty milk bottle on her stoop, look around to see what was going on, and pull her head back in like a snail. When she heard another sound, she would repeat the performance taking the bottle back *in*.

As far as we knew, she used the same empty bottle for years. She never said a word. We and our four children always gave her a big, friendly "hello". This caused her sour looks to curdle.

Sometimes we would come out of our apartment singly at thirty-second intervals so that we could watch the performance.

She got her kicks, though. The aforementioned kindergarten had a playground just beneath her window. When the happy laughter and terrified cries became too loud, she would call this institution on the phone and ask to speak to "the Warden of the Children's Insane Asylum".

Our lives proceeded calmly. A drawing I had done of our elevator operator was reproduced in the Sunday *Times*, and he was in ecstasy for a few days, as all the tenants asked him to autograph their copies. During this period, I was constantly painting covers for *Time* magazine, but my children were not impressed. After all, one of their friend's fathers was doing the covers for *Superman Comics*.

Bizarre things began to happen. We noticed unusual activities in the house across the street. The owners were very wealthy, and through the windows

48

we could see their extravagant goings-on. The parents would go away quite often and leave their teenage children in charge. One day an entire truckload of easels and paint boxes was delivered, and the cheerful youngsters transformed the top story into an "authentic artist's studio". They then invited all their friends, who sat on the floor and drank wine, no doubt imagining themselves to be characters from *La Boheme*.

One night, about four in the morning, I awoke to the sounds of a hubbub in the street below.

"What's that?" Marjorie mumbled in her sleep.

I staggered to the window and looked out. I saw several young men wearing jackets and ties, surrounding another young man, who was laughing hysterically. I couldn't see what the others were doing, but the lone youth broke loose, ran fifteen yards, and *stopped*. He turned and laughed some more while the others approached him slowly and once more closed in upon him. After a minute he got loose again and repeated his actions.

"What's happening now?" asked Marjorie.

"It seems to be some sort of college initiation," I replied. We both went back to sleep.

On the following day, we found out that the man was being stabbed. Hysteria had caused him to stop, turn, and laugh. According to the newspaper, he had started smashing windows further down the block. This property damage called attention to his plight, and his assailants had fled.

"Why didn't you call the police?" asked Marjorie.

"Because the guy was laughing all the time," I replied guiltily. "But I'll never let this happen again."

Life proceeded on our street. We watched the "5:30 Car Switching Club" at work every morning. Alternate-side-of-the-street parking created strange practices. Many of the car owners on our block had banded together to outwit the expensive garages and parking lots. Just before the 6 p.m. deadline (after which parking was allowed on both sides til morning) a designated member of the club (with all the keys) would move each car to the opposite and empty side. On the following day, another member would move them all back.

Once a cop appeared at 5:45 and started ticketing the criminal vehicles. It was fun watching the designate desperately moving the cars while the policeman gleefully wrote out tickets. Then (after 6:00) our weary friend gamely transferred them all *back* again.

On weekends the lucky occupants had 62 hours of free parking. New Yorkers have been known to cancel fabulous weekend plans rather than lose such a plum.

One evening I was sitting reading in our apartment. Marjorie and her sister were at the window.

"My God," said Marjorie, "Someone just jumped out of a car and hit an old lady over the head."

I hurried to the window and saw the sad, crumpled figure. I also saw dozens of heads popping out of all the other windows. This time I *didn't* hesitate. I rushed to the phone and dialed "O".

"Quick," I said, "Give me the police. I want to report a murder."

"What precinct are you in?" asked the operator in a flat voice.

"I don't know," I shouted frantically. "This poor old lady has been murdered."

"I'll get you my supervisor," she said tartly.

"What seems to be the trouble?" asked the next voice.

I repeated my story and gave my address. Finally I got through.

"What's *your* name and where do you live?" asked the policeman. He seemed surprised when I told him.

Within three minutes a police car and ambulance arrived and took the poor woman away. She died during the night. Her purse had been snatched by the assailants. It had contained a little over six dollars.

The next afternoon, two plainclothes detectives came to our apartment, no doubt observed by the little old lady putting out (or taking in) that battered bottle.

"We want to speak to Robert Vickrey about this murder." they said.

"He's not here. He's at work," said Marjorie.

"We'll wait 'til he comes home," they said.

"But he works 'til eleven o'clock at night," she said.

"We go off duty at six," was the reply.

"But he's only two and a half blocks away," said Marjorie. "And besides, he didn't see it. *I* did."

"Our orders were to come here and talk to Robert Vickrey," they said firmly.

Marjorie sighed. "By the way," she asked, "did anyone else call in about this?"

"No," they said.

Later in the afternoon the kids came home from "The Children's Insane Asylum" and the policemen played with them for a couple of hours, showing off their badges and guns. Promptly at six, the two lawmen left. We never heard from them again.

"Are those nice cops coming back?" asked the kids. "They certainly were a lot of fun."

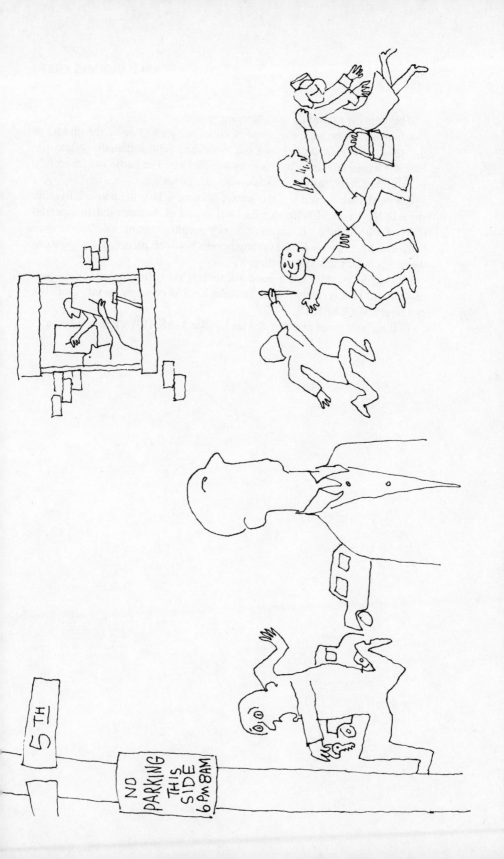

"Murder isn't funny," said Marjorie grimly.

After this, when we came home at night, we walked down the middle of the street and then *darted* into our doorway, falling thankfully into the elevator where our celebrity operator was dozing. The bottle lady evidently went to bed early, so we couldn't wish her goodnight.

Eventually we moved to the country. Sometime later the house across the street in New York blew up. A naked girl ran out of the ruins and disappeared down Fifth Avenue. It seems that our wealthy young neighbors were "Weathermen", who were building bombs between parties. I always wondered about that naked girl, though.

My son Sean, who has a good vocabulary (but isn't too strong on pronunciation) said recently, "Life in New York is certainly weird, Dad. It's positively MAKABRAY."

"I think you mean macabre," I said, "But MAKABRAY says it better."

PAINTING JFK

THE Voice from *Time* said, "John Kennedy will be on a plane between Chicago and Cleveland next week. He's willing to pose."

"On a plane," I said nervously.

"Yes," said the voice, "He's going to make a speech at the Annual Cleveland Steer Roast." Then quickly the voice continued, "And it's a *great* honor. He's never been willing to pose before."

It was 1960. After working for *Time* for many years, I was used to sudden, mind-wrenching trips to Paris, Morocco, St. Louis, and other such exotic places. However, I had never worked on a plane before.

"Well, I won't try to paint him, but I'll sketch him and take some pictures, if that will be OK,"

This was about a month before Kennedy was elected. He was very busy with his campaign.

A few days later I woke up in Chicago and, after looking at my watch, found that I had overslept. I rushed to the airport to discover that I was really an hour and two minutes early as I had neglected to reset my watch for the proper time zone the night before. This was brought to my rather sleepy attention by the *Timeman* who had been assigned to cover the campaign. He also briefed me on the fact that I must hide my camera when I boarded Kennedy's plane, since all the other members of the press would be upset if they found out that a member of the third estate had been allowed on the *Caroline*.

I skulked onto the aircraft, bending over to hide my criminal evidence beneath a raincoat, somewhat like the stricken male characters in *Lysistrata*. After mumbling forcedly cheerful "hellos" to several people who did not look up, I settled down in a seat to brood a bit and ponder the fact that I had had no breakfast. But we were on the way to a steer roast, after all.

53

Through the window I could see Senator Kennedy approaching, and I immediately began studying his facial planes. He entered, and again nobody looked up. *That* made me feel a little better. He strode down the aisle and took a seat at the front. Soon we were aloft.

"Remember," someone whispered to me, "anything you hear is strictly off the record."

Realizing that I might be about to overhear information that would sway the course of nations, and feeling a knot of tension (or hunger) in my stomach, I approached the Senator. His staff was coaching him on the different types of TV makeup. I sketched for a few rather bumpy minutes and then was introduced to him. He was friendly but seemed withdrawn and slightly upset.

Finally he asked, "Aren't you rather young for this?"

At the time I was 34, but people told me I appeared much younger. Over the next few days I thought of many brilliant and pithy references to his own relative youth, but at the time I only mumbled something like "not really."

After a pause, he asked quietly, "Who else have you painted for *Time*?"

Not wanting to mention the 16 covers I had done, I replied succinctly, "Well . . . Lyndon Johnson."

There was a long, cold silence, and then someone said we had better get on with the posing.

Since most of the seats had desks in front of them, I had to lie across one of these to take closeups of his face. Also I found that my light meter was broken. Eventually, with someone holding up a copy of the *New York Times* to reflect light into the shadows of his face (with those difficult planes), I rolled around on the desk and managed to get a few pictures. He seemed very tired and distant and I felt that only S. J. Perelman could have done justice to the scene, as the aircraft hit a bump, a cloud blotted out the light, or the *New York Times* slipped.

When the session was over, I retired to my seat and asked if there was any food on the plane. My question was greeted by an enigmatic smile. I did a few more shaky drawings, and then we landed.

I slunk off the plane with my illegal camera and got on the press bus that was to follow the Senator in the motorcade. Again, I tried to hide my photographic equipment from the members of the working press who looked at me with suspicion. A few minutes later the press bus became separated from the Senator's car, and the reporters were very upset.

"Suppose something happened to him," said one. "We would not be able to get any pictures."

To this day I am chilled by that remark.

Eventually the bus caught up with the Senator and everyone breathed a sigh of relief.

We wound our way through Cleveland and to a park on the outskirts of town where the Steer Roast was under way. Kennedy was rushed through the crowd by his cohorts while I trotted breathlessly (and hungrily) behind.

I'll eat after the speech while he shakes hands and mingles with the crowd, I told myself cheerfully.

I stood at the base of platform where he was talking and consoled myself by noticiing that his shoes (a few inches from my eyes) were in worse shape than mine. As soon as the Senator stepped before the crowd, the tired and withdrawn attitudes completely dropped away, and he became a truly charismatic figure. His words, however, were drowned out for me by the rumbling of my stomach. He finished and strode from the platform to great applause.

I followed in a leisurely manner looking for a roasting steer, or at least a popcorn stand. Soon I noticed that the entire motorcade and press bus were leaving without me. Here I was in a strange city with very little money, no plane ticket, no press card, no credit card (remember way back then?) —in short, no life support system.

A car decked with flags caught my eye and I explained my plight to the driver, who did not seem interested until I mentioned the magic word, *Time*. After a hurried discussion the man told me to jump into the car and with a great flurry of flags and sirens, we roared off toward the airport, passing several roast beef sandwich stands on the way. From the pursuant conversation it became clear that I was taking a State Senator and a Congressman considerably out of their way in order to put me on my plane. Such is the power of the word, *Time*.

At the airport I was hurried onto the press plane with my camera now insolently in sight. As we took off into the evening air, I once again posed my tedious question. No, I was told there was no food on the plane, but I could have all the martinis I could drink. Safe with the knowledge that, after all, alcohol is a food, I careened toward the East after my day in the life of John Fitzgerald Kennedy.

At home in my studio I began the portrait, and it soon became clear that it was not going well. The facial planes seemed to change from every different angle. The eyes seemed taut with pain even though the mouth was cheerful. His upper eyelids drooped in an unattractive way. In short, the features of this handsome face were not individually attractive. My wife thought he looked too sad. My son, Scott, thought that he looked about to burst into laughter. The only thing anybody liked was the hair. The painting was a failure.

When I delivered it to *Time*, the managing editor said nothing. He commissioned another artist to do the cover from a publicity photograph. My painting was returned to me several years later with no comment in a plain brown wrapper.

CARDINAL CUSHING AT 7:30 A.M.

I PAINTED many religious leaders for *Time*, but one of the most interesting was the late Cardinal Cushing. He posed for me in 1964 during the Republican Convention. With triumphant glee the Voice from *Time* had earlier announced that the Cardinal would give me three sittings of two hours apiece. Each would start at 7:30 a.m. For anyone who knows my sleeping and working habits, this would be the equivalent of telling Dracula to come to the Boston Common at high noon.

When I told my wife about the upcoming event, she said, "Great! I'll come with you. I can catch the Republican Convention."

We got someone to take care of the children and we hurried up to Boston to stay at a motel in the vicinity of the Cardinal's headquarters. It wasn't very fancy, but it *was* near the great man. I figured that we would be free after 9:30 each day to see shows, movies, and art exhibits. Naturally we would be eating at Boston's best restaurants . . . on my charge account. Immediately after we checked in, Marjorie turned on the television and began to watch the so-called "Goldwater Convention."

"Let's go to dinner," I suggested.

"No, no," she said. "This is much more interesting."

Eventually we had a quick bite at some nearby bistro and hurried back to the television.

"I don't want to lose my cool," I said to Marjorie. "I wonder if I have to kiss his ring."

She was not listening.

Even with my insomnia, I finally became sleepy. And besides, I had to get up at 6 a.m.

"Can't we turn off the television?" I pleaded.

58

"No," she replied. "We have to see the reruns."

I dozed fitfully through the complicated political machinations and was eventually awakened by the requested shrill phone call. Marjorie slept late. After all, she needed her strength for the ordeal ahead. I had a light breakfast and hurried to the Cardinal's office.

He was a truly charismatic man with a wonderful gravelly voice—and a great face. Sadly, he was very ill and was living on custard and bottled oxygen.

And he *didn't* expect me to kiss his ring.

I had requested that a reporter interview my subject so that I would be able to see a variety of expressions on his face. As we rode up in the elevator, the Timeman (I was Timeartist Vickrey) noticed that there was no button for the top floor—only a keyhole.

"That's where the nuns live," announced our host with a sly smile. "I'm not allowed to have a key to *that* floor."

The portrait sitting went well, and afterward the Cardinal took us on a tour. He showed us drawers and closets full of impressive vestments. He denigrated all this pomp and circumstance, but a twinkle in his eye belied his statements. He was enjoying himself immensely.

Later I returned to the motel and saw a bit more of the convention.

"We can have a quick lunch," said Marjorie. "But we must get back immediately."

That evening, once again, I suggested that we have a good dinner and see a movie.

"No, we might miss something," said Marjorie.

We had a precipitous, local meal—and then back to you-know-what. My stomach was beginning to churn. Finally I fell asleep to the dulcet sounds of political oratory, surely one of the world's great soporifics.

I was groggily on duty at 7:30 the next morning and found my subject even more likeable than before. Halfway through the sitting/interview he started to reminisce about the Kennedys.

"I'm not a great friend of theirs," he said. "I wish the press would not keep stating that I am. I'm their priest and nothing more."

Meanwhile, back at the motel, things were heating up.

"Fantastic!" shouted Marjorie. "This is the most fantastic thing I've ever seen."

I pleaded again for the usual, but yes, yes . . . I know . . . we would miss the reruns. I fell asleep with the customary sounds in my ears and the usual churning in my stomach. Marjorie nudged me awake an hour later.

"You have got to see what they are doing to Rockefeller," she said.
"Are they making him lose his cool?" I mumbled as I drifted back to fitful sleep.

The next morning I arose unsteadily and decided that a really good breakfast might settle my stomach. I kissed Marjorie as I left, but she only mumbled, "No, Barry, no."

In the coffee shop I had orange juice, pancakes, bacon, and lots of coffee. Dracula could not have enjoyed his blood feast more.

The sitting was going very well, and so far I was keeping my cool. My subject was outlining his philosophy of life, when suddenly my stomach told me that I only had a minute to go in a countdown to catastrophe. I politely excused myself to visit the Cardinal's private bathroom. I turned the faucets in the sink on full force, knelt down, and not only lost my cool, but everything else. After this, I rinsed out my mouth with the Cardinal's mouthwash, went back, and finished the portrait. Everyone agreed that the sittings had gone well.

I returned to Marjorie and announced that we could go home. But, of course, she pointed out, we would miss part of the convention. I suggested we could hear it on the radio in the car.

"All right," said Marjorie. "As long as we can see the reruns tonight."

A POLITICAL HERO—ALMOST

I ONCE painted a portrait of a young student leader whom we shall call Charles Smith.

It all began in 1964.

"We want you to paint a picture which will sum up the whole black youth movement in the South," said the Voice from *Time*.

"Great," I said.

"We'll work out your itinerary," said the voice.

"I'd like to go too," said Marjorie.

Eventually we flew to Columbia, North Carolina.

"Try not to get lynched," our conservative parents warned us.

"O.K.," we said, waving farewell.

We checked into the best hotel in Columbia, where we met the *Time* stringer for the area. A stringer is someone who usually works with the local paper but can do occasional jobs on the side for major publications. This man tried to be friendly, but kept muttering about "damned Northerners." However, he was good at his job, and he arranged for several sittings with Charles Smith.

Then the first problem arose. No black person was allowed above the first floor of the hotel. The desk clerk mumbled his lines to me.

"No cuh-boys above this floor."

"No what?" I asked, not understanding.

"No c-boys," he whispered behind his hand.

"Cowboys? We have no cowboys," I exclaimed loudly and naively.

The stringer stepped in hastily to interpret. Charles Smith was waiting patiently a few feet away.

61

"Could we dress him up as a bellboy?" asked the stringer, looking over his shoulder.

Charles Smith nodded his willingness.

"We have no colored bellboys," announced the clerk triumphantly.

So we all moved to a nearby two-story motel that allowed blacks on the second floor. This establishment also featured a swimming pool with a plastic bubble over it. Our stringer then left us to our mysterious Northern customs. Shortly afterward, Charles Smith came to pose. He seemed to be a careful, likeable and nervous youth of about 21. He was an ordained minister, as was his father.

The sittings progressed smoothly. I painted him next to the motel window. The people passing on the balcony were startled to see him in such sacrosanct territory.

We had our noonday meal at a stand-up lunch counter. In those days a white person was willing to masticate *standing* next to a black person—but not *sitting* next to one. This moral dilemma was solved in many places by removing the seats.

Back at the motel, Marjorie asked, "Who's that strange man standing down there looking so sinister?"

"I don't know," I said.

"He's there all the time now," said Marjorie.

"I wonder what they would say if I swam in the pool," mused Charles.

"You're braver than I am if you do," I said.

"That strange looking man is still there," said Marjorie. "He hasn't looked this way, but he's been there for hours."

"Would you like to come home for dinner," asked Charles after the sitting.

"Sure," we said.

We had a delightful time at his parents' home. They were proud of him, but felt that his civil disobedience was interfering with school work.

"Marks come first," said his father.

"But, Dad, I'm going to be on the cover of *Time*," said Charles.

"First things come first," said his father sternly.

As we were waiting outside for the car to drive us back to our liberal motel, Charles's mother said, "Don't stand under the light."

"Why?" I asked naively.

She shook her head.

"That man is in the courtyard again," said Marjorie on the following day.

"Let's go to a restaurant for dinner," said Charles.

"O.K.," I said. "But not tonight. We're having dinner with the stringer."
Charles looked hurt, as if we were making up an excuse for not dining
with him publicly.

"But let's do it tomorrow," I said quickly, catching the vibration.
He cheered up.

"Where shall we eat?" Marjorie and I asked.

"There's only one place in town that will serve us," said Charles. "The
airport. It's federal property."

First, however, we had dinner with the stringer and his wife, who obviously disapproved of our politics. They picked a restaurant which was far
away from Columbia. We had to bring our own liquor in a brown bag
because of state laws. The restaurant they had chosen was small and dark.
They evidently wanted to go to a place where they would not be recognized.
We felt our way to our seats, clutching our bottles.

"How do they charge us for our drinks?" I asked.

"You'll see," they said grimly.

We placed the bottles on the floor next to our chairs. The house supplied
the mixers, the glasses and the ice. When we wanted a drink we had to
reach down, pick up the bottle (still in the bag) and pour it into our glasses.
The waiter made a note each time we did this and charged us the same
amount as if we were drinking at the Stork Club.

The next night, as planned, we went to dinner at the airport. Charles
showed up with a beautiful blonde, evidently hoping to shock us. It didn't
and even the hostess wasn't shocked. She seated all four of us.

"You notice she didn't smile, though," said Charles. "By the way, I
can't pose tomorrow morning," he added "I'm conducting a service at my
church."

"We'd like to come," said Marjorie and I.

"O.K.," he said dubiously. "But the place is rather primitive. You may
be uncomfortable."

We all drove to the church which was quite far out in the country. Charles
couldn't let us in because he didn't have the key.

"I'm not sure who has it," he said. "Remember, there's no electricity
and no plumbing."

Soon the deacon arrived with the key, followed by members of the congregation. Charles introduced us to many of them. All the men fumbled
their hats off their heads before shaking hands with us, a gesture to break
the heart of a Northern liberal. They also waited cautiously to see if *we*
would make the first gesture to shake hands.

Once inside, we said, "We'll just sit quietly in the back."

"No," said Charles firmly.

He placed us in the middle of the front row. In 1964, it was an honor for a black congregation to have white visitors.

The service began. It was one of the most beautiful we had ever attended, and we told Charles so. He looked embarrassed.

"I'm sure you found it very colorful," he said with friendly bitterness.

The next day I finished the portrait. Our friend in the courtyard was back on duty. As we left, I walked up and stood close to him.

"I think the sittings went very well, Charles." I said in a loud voice.

Our friend just kept looking off into space. I shrugged my shoulders.

As all three of us left our stand-up luncheon that day, we ran into one of Charles's friends. The four of us chatted briefly. I felt a strange hostility in the air.

Later Charles said to us, "You see, a few weeks ago he was the big political fat cat around here. When I appear on the cover of *Time*, *I* will be the fat cat."

Several months later on the date when Charles's cover was suposed to appear, Khrushchev broke the atomic test ban.

Guess who was on Time's cover.

DINNER IN ORLEANS

PAUL Fussell has written a wonderful book titled *Class*. It's very funny and very perceptive. I've bought several copies and am giving it to my friends (I hope they remain my friends). Mr. Fussell dissects all frailties and pretensions with great skill, pinning us up for inspection the way a lepidopterist does his butterflies. Every item in our homes is an indication of our ineffectual striving to achieve "class".

Paul is completely fair, however. He looks down on *everybody*.

Never again will I wear my sports shirt collar outside my jacket collar. And I am trying to force myself to pronounce "gourmet" with the accent on the last syllable.

In the appendix we are given a check list by which each of us can ascertain his own class level by examining his living room. For example:

Hardwood floor	add 4
Parquet floor	add 8
Vinyl floor	subtract 6
Cellophane on any lamp shade	subtract 4
Motorcycle kept in livingroom	subtract 10
Potted palm tree	add 5
Bowling ball carrier	subtract 6
Fringe on any upholstered furniture	subtract 4

Add these up and your score will indicate your class level.

All this reminds me of my first encounter with Paul and Betty Fussell many, many years ago when Marjorie and I were invited to dinner at their house. Toby and Tom were also invited. Paul was not present, but was expected momentarily.

"This will be a real gourmet feast," whispered Marjorie, alas, putting the accent on the first syllable.

But then, again *I* was wearing my sports shirt collar outside my jacket collar. The motif of the meal evidently was the color white. The soup was off-white, the filet of sole was served with white sauce, the chocolate mousse was (of course) white. Each item was delicious, and it was only later that I realized no teeth were required for any dish. At this point Paul was still due momentarily.

The high point of the festivities came when the guests were given the problem of guessing the ingredients of the pale soup. Everything from kumquats to rare curds were suggested. But Betty smiled negatively until we were forced to admit defeat.

Then she triumphantly announced, "turtle stock."

Little moans of "Oh, yes," and "I should have guessed" escaped from the lips of the celebrants.

Then Toby announced grandly, "This has been one of my *two* soup experiences."

Tom and I exchanged quick glances. We were both wondering if we were going to get something to sink our teeth into. I was beginning to feel a strange prickling sensation between my shoulder blades.

I was to learn at a later date that Betty was a well-known gour*met* cook who had had Craig Claiborne to dinner (and he reviewed it in his column —favorably, of course). I also found out that Paul was a brilliant scholar and writer, author-to-be of such works as "Theory of Prosody in Eighteenth-Century England" and "The Thetorical World of Augustan Humanism: Ethics and Imagery from Swift to Burke." At this point in our dinner he was still expected momentarily.

Anyway the whole evening was delightful. We decided to get the same group together in a month at our house on Tonset Road. We set the date and left.

Paul was still due shortly . . .

Three weeks later our stove was condemned and was removed from our house, leaving a large blank spot on the kitchen floor. We were told that we would have to wait several weeks for a new one. Naturally, we decided to call off the party. However, no one knew how to reach the Fussells, who were away. Marjorie and I figured that most people double check on a party planned that far in advance, so we didn't worry about it.

Safe in the arms of this misconception, I was sitting on our porch on the appointed day when I saw the Fussells drive up. I quickly ran inside, went into the bedroom and on the telephone, reinvited everybody. Marjorie said she would think of something.

Finally we were all assembled. I had recently bought a tape recorder, and someone suggested that we tape some of Tom's excellent poetry and then get each person to speak his comments into the machine. Tom, of course, would read the poems. We would then have a record of this cultural event. Toby, his wife Aubrey, and Betty made scholarly comments into the microphone. Paul didn't say much. He just sat looking like his picture on the dust jacket of *Class*. Once again I began to feel a strange prickling sensation between my shoulder blades.

I have always had a tin ear for poetry and didn't feel qualified to make any sensible comments on Tom's work. Tom, of course, knew this. When it came my turn to speak into the microphone I decided to satirize my lack of accomplishment in this area. Therefore, I discussed only the sound levels of the tape machine, making such comments as "the third poem was my favorite because the little needle did not go into the red so often."

As we finished the tape Betty hissed into my ear, "Either you and Tom are very good friends or you are a complete. . . . ." . . . and here she used Lyndon Johnson's favorite expletive.

Lamely, I mumbled something about its being the former, but by then she had swept by me into the dining area where Marjorie, who had quietly gone out and come back, was presenting the assembly with five very complicated pizzas.

The locks of Medusa could not have brought forth more stony stares than were evident on the faces of the Fussells.

Now that I have read Paul's book I know that pizza is the sign that one is beyond all hope, and I know that the prickling sensation between my shoulder blades was the sting of the lepidopterist's pin. The party broke up early that night, the Fussells now *both* looking like the picture on the back of Paul's book.

We haven't seen them since.

DINNER IN DENNISPORT

A FEW years ago Marjorie and I were invited to a dinner party in Dennisport. I will call our hosts Harriet and Leonard Hostile. This is to let you know I have changed their names. The reason will soon become clear. All the other names and events are accurate.

We had known the Hostiles for years. Leonard was a vice president of a tobacco company. Harriet was a self-styled mystic and believer in reincarnation.

"Bring all your friends," said Harriet. "We've invited more than a hundred people. It should be the biggest bash in the history of Dennisport."

We knew these two had alienated almost everyone in town at some point. They seemed to feel the insult was the friendly form of human contact, and they had made many such contacts.

"By the way," said Harriet, "it's a costume party. Try to think of something really wild."

Marjorie and I lined up as many people as possible . . . with little luck. Two friends agreed to come if they could wear Ku Klux Klan outfits, thus mocking our hosts' right-wing politics. Another couple accepted on the condition that they not wear *any* costumes. Marjorie and I wore pajamas and bathrobes as a hint that we would rather be home in bed.

The six of us drove to the Hostiles' waterfront house, expecting to be lost in the vast crowd of revelers. When we arrived, we found that, except for the couple next door, we were the only guests.

The party was catered by two very dignified black ladies who stood next to huge tureens of steaming food, looking very sternly at our friends in their Ku Klux Klan getups.

"Where is everybody?" we asked naively.

"They'll be here shortly," announced Harriet, who was dressed as one of her previous incarnations—a queen of ancient Egypt.

"Nobody is showing up," whispered the couple next door. "Harriet and Leonard have insulted everybody in town."

Leonard, who was well over six feet tall and weighed close to 300 pounds, galloped into view. He was dressed as a . . . well, let's say he was the part that was left over after the Godfather's gang put the horse's head in the movie producer's bed. He was ensconced like a huge beetle in a purple rump with an orange tail. He had purchased his costume at a joke-and-magic store. He asked us what we wanted to drink and flicked his tail in our faces saucily as he left. Later, when the ladies wished to smoke, he gallantly gave them a light . . . with exploding matches.

Joy reigned supreme for an hour or two, although the caterers avoided passing the hors d'oeuvres to our KKK-costumed friends. Harriet took pictures of all these festivities with her Instamatic Flash. Eventually Leonard passed out, and the four men present (one per limb) carried him up to bed.

Harriet continued to take photographs. The remaining nine of us tried to make a dent in the vast sea of food and drink.

"Why did you come in such unimaginative costumes?" asked Harriet, looking at our pajamas and bathrobes.

We said nothing. She took some more pictures.

Then Leonard came crashing down the stairs again, flicking his orange tail to express his anger at having been put to bed prematurely. Harriet sighed. The caterers glowered at the KKK costumes. Leonard made a few passes at the female guests . . . and passed out again. Marjorie yawned. The four men carried our host back to his room. It was difficult carrying half a horse up the narrow stairs.

"Now comes the climax," crooned our hostess, deep in the arms of John Begg. "I'm going to throw all the used flash bulbs into the Sound. They light up, you know, when they hit the salt water. It's a beautiful, beautiful sight."

"No, no," we all pleaded. "Think of the children's feet with all that broken glass."

"All right then," said Harriet. "I'll throw them in all by myself."

Thinking fast, I rushed into the kitchen and whispered to the startled caterers. "Quick, give me all the little white objects in the room."

I wadded up small balls of wet paper towels and broke off little slivers of soap. The two ladies watched me with shocked horror as I jammed all these into my *left* bathrobe pocket. I then returned to the orgy in the living room.

"Down to the beach," shouted Harriet.

Everyone looked very angry as Harriet and I headed seaward. She handed me all the used flashbulbs, which I thrust into my *right* bathrobe pocket.

At the water's edge I called out cheerfully, "I'll throw them in."

I grabbed handfuls of soap and wet paper towels from my left pocket. Like Thor hurling thunderbolts, I flung them far into the water.

"See, I told you," cried Harriet. "They're all lighting up."

After these ecstatic moments, Harriet and I climbed the hill back up to the house. I expected to be greeted as a returning hero, but instead, the mothers descended upon me in a body, cursing me loudly. One of them started pummeling me.

Ineffectually defending myself, I cried, "I'm innocent! Your children's feet are safe."

At least that's what I was trying to say. Finally I led the mothers into the kitchen and had my story confirmed by the caterers. I'm not sure anyone believed me.

We wended our way home shortly afterward. I drove very carefully. I didn't want the police to stop our car full of people in pajamas and KKK outfits.

A HOSTILE NEW YEAR'S EVE

"**Y**OU kids are so unsophisticated," said Harriet Hostile to Marjorie and me. "Your idea of an evening out is to have dinner and see a Bergman movie. Leonard and I want to show you what life is really about."

At this point we had moved out of New York City and were living in Connecticut.

"Come in during the day and we'll take you out for a really fabulous New Year's Eve."

We arrived around noon.

"Marjorie and I are going shopping," said Harriet. "Leonard wants to take Bob to meet his staff."

The time was approximately 1962, and Leonard was vice president, in charge of radio and TV advertising, for a major tobacco company. This was somewhat equivalent to being executive officer on the *Titanic*, since all cigarette ads were banned from these media shortly afterward.

"I'm producing a new show called *Mr. Citizen*," said Leonard. "I want you to meet my gang and tell me what you think of the pilot. I want *real* integrity. These guys are all 'yes' men. Tear it to pieces, if you want. Don't pull any punches."

"Umm," I said.

As we left, Harriet whispered in my ear, "Say, you like it, no matter how rotten it is. After all, *you* just paint pictures. *Leonard* must perform miracles every day."

True to the stereotype, most of the advertising executives *did* look worried.

After the showing, Leonard announced, "Bob, here, has real integrity. He's going to tell you the truth about the show. Go ahead, Bob."

"Well," I said, clearing my throat at some length. "I thought it was . . .

really great. Of course, there were a few minor things that bothered me. Very minor.''

The staff looked glum. Like a tightrope walker I weaved my way between truth and tact.

"See" said Leonard. "Bob has real integrity. He tells it like it is."

"Who is this creep?" the expression on the faces of the staff seemed to say.

"That ought to shake 'em up a bit," said Leonard as we left. "Now, let's go home and have a few drinks before we go to the Stork Club."

Back at the Hostile duplex the inbibing began.

"Marjorie is no fun to go shopping with," said Harriet. "She never buys anything she doesn't need."

I was silent. Harriet served us some delicious canapés.

"What is this spread?" I asked.

"That's my secret," she said with her Mona Lisa smile.

"How come you're not drinking your usual Cutty Sark?" I asked.

"My doctor says I'm too thin. I should eat more potatoes. So I've switched from scotch to vodka."

"These canapés really are great," I said.

After a few more drinks and a political discussion, Leonard, as usual, became quite cantankerous.

"We don't allow Commies in our house," he bellowed.

Marjorie and I defended our political position.

"Commies, Democrats, what's the difference?" he countered as he physically thrust me out of the front door onto the cobblestoned street.

Because he was well over six and a half feet tall and weighed about 300 pounds, I said nothing."

"Wait for me," Marjorie called timidly.

Leonard turned back and headed for the Cutty Sark.

"That's just the liquor talking," said Harried, shooing us back in. "Have some more canapés."

"I will if you tell me what's in them?" I said taking two and starting to munch.

"O.K.," she said and whispered in my ear.

I replaced the extra delicacy when she wasn't looking.

At about nine o'clock the private limousine from the Stork Club arrived.

"Good night honey. We love you," they called out to their teenage son, Leonard Jr., who made no reply.

As we entered the hallowed halls, Leonard checked to make sure that the package of cigarettes in the window was *his* brand!

"We used to supply the Stork Club with *real* cigarettes," he commented. "But some jerk always stole them. Now we send them packages full of balsa wood."

"I hope Sherman will sit at our table tonight," mused Harriet wistfully.

"Who's Sherman?" I asked naively.

"Sherman Billingsley—the owner. Oh, Bob, you're so unsophisticated," said Harriet.

"I wonder if he'll bring the twenty-five-year-old bottle of scotch to the table?" said Leonard. "If he really likes you, he tells the waiter to put it on your table and you can have all you want."

"I don't like scotch," I said. "Does he have a twenty-five-year-old bottle of gin?"

The dinner, which would cost five or six hundred dollars these days, began. Sherman Billingsley walked in—but he merely waved to us across the room.

"Is he mad at us, do you suppose?" asked Harriet in a worried voice.

"I can't think of anything we've done," said Leonard looking puzzled.

At about 10:30, a hush fell over the celebrants as an elderly, bald man walked in and sat near us.

"That's Walter Winchell," said Harriet in a worshipful voice.

"I didn't recognize him without his hat," said Marjorie.

Sherman passed again—and sat at *another* table. Harriet and Leonard looked crestfallen. Leonard offered Harriet a cigarette.

"My doctor says I should cut down on my smoking. The old TB, you know." she said.

"Don't you dare," growled Leonard lighting one and placing it in her mouth.

The waiters started passing out funny hats and noisemakers.

We said, "No thank you."

Leonard caught Walter Winchell's eye and gave him a little wave. The great man stared at his plate.

Soon it was time for dessert.

"Is the strawberry shortcake made with a cake or a biscuit?" I asked.

"How would you like it?" asked the waiter.

"A biscuit," I said.

He hurried away.

"He's going to make a biscuit just for you," said Leonard. "He knows us."

"Here comes Sherman," chortled Harriet.

He sat down.

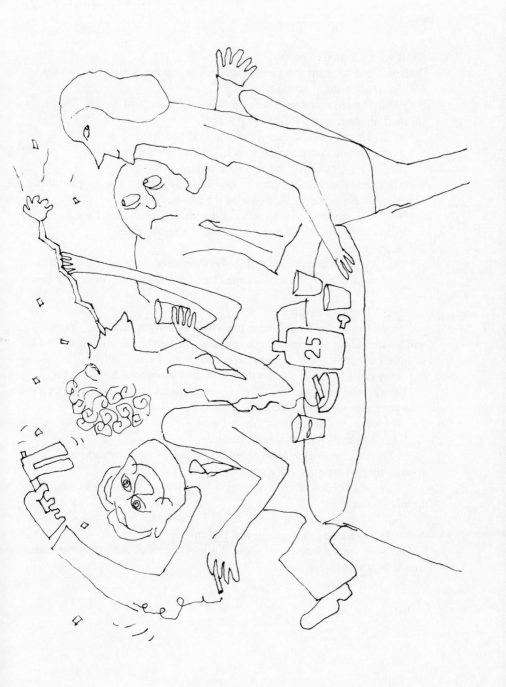

"Boy, am I tired," he said.

Harriet and Leonard tried to engage him in conversation.

"I'm *really* tired," he said.

Leonard hinted about the twenty-five-year-old bottle of scotch. Sherman snapped his fingers and the elixir appeared.

"Well, I gotta go now. See you." he said and left.

"I thought you had given up scotch," said Leonard to Harriet.

"This is an occasion," she replied groggily.

At midnight the orchestra played *Auld Lang Syne* and a few people called out "Happy New Year" and sounded their noisemakers.

"There's a twenty percent surcharge for this music," said Leonard.

"Wasn't it worth it?" whispered Harriet triumphantly.

I yawned.

"Oh, you're so unsophisticated," she murmured once more as we left.

"By the way, there's a few canapés left. Would you like some?" asked Harriet.

"No," I replied hastily.

"Now, Bob, you sleep alone in the hide-a-bed in the basement. Marjorie and I will sleep in the master bedroom, and big Leonard is already out cold in little Leonard's room," said Harriet, like a cruise director.

"Why can't Marjorie sleep with me in the hide-a-bed? It's a double."

Harriet smiled profoundly, "Nobody is allowed to have sex in this house if anyone else is on the premises."

"We weren't planning anything," I said.

"House rules," replied Harriet firmly.

As I was drifting off to lonely slumber, Harriet swept unsteadily into the room with two aspirins and a glass of water.

"This will keep you from having a hangover," she said, kissing me lightly on the brow.

"But I've never had one in my life," I protested.

"Bob, poor Bob," she murmured patronizingly as she left.

Oh, yes, you're wondering about the ingredients of the canapé spread: one-half peanut butter—one half ketchup.

DINNER WITH THE DUKE AND DUCHESS OF WINDSOR

MY father used to tell me at great length about his years as an undergraduate at Annapolis. He hoped that I would eventually attend that fine institution. Anyone who knows me would understand that this would be like issuing an invitation to Dante to spend four years in the inferno.

My father always felt that he had indirectly helped Eisenhower to be elected president. You see, he and Ike had taken the Kansas entry exam to Annapolis at the same time. Only two candidates from each state could be accepted. My father's marks (and one other man's) were higher than Ike's. Thus, our president-to-be did not go to Annapolis. Later he took the exam for West Point—and made it.

Until Jimmy Carter, no Annapolis candidate had ever been elected president. But lots of West Point men *did* go on to the White House. Think about it. For want of a nail, the shoe . . . etc.

Anyway, back to Maryland in 1913. My father used to date a lovely young lady named Wallis Warfield. One night he took her to the Annapolis prom. When he went to pick her up at her home, he found that she had been unable to fasten the catches on the back of her formal gown. He was fumbling with these when her mother came in.

"I'll bet you wouldn't be so clumsy if you were *un*doing those things," she chuckled.

The festivities were well under way, when my father and his date retired into the recesses of the Navy gymnasium to discuss the metric system . . . or some such thing. Being a perfect gentlemen he would never tell me what went on during that interlude. Suffice it is to say that when they came back to the dance floor, the band and the dancers were gone, the lights were off, and the building was locked.

My father was a great conversationalist.

In those days, when a young man and his girl were locked in a building overnight, she was compromised, and they had to get married. Eventually my father and Wallis found an unlocked window and escaped not only from the gymnasium, but from the concomitant obligations. If all the windows had been locked, think of the outcome. For want of . . .

Forty years pass, and it's now 1960. Our friends, Maggie and Paul, have invited Marjorie and me to join them for dinner at Maude Chez Elle, a fabulous French restaurant then on 53rd Street in New York City.

"The food is great! And the service is the best in town," chortled Maggie.

"Mais oui," said Paul.

We arrived at the establishment and were ushered to our table by a large obsequious staff.

"I told you," said Maggie, "the *best* service in town."

We had a leisurely drink, and then in walked Edward Arnold, who was greeted by *twice* as many obsequious minions, and he obviously felt that he deserved it.

"I hope the whole staff doesn't wait on *him*," whispered Maggie.

"Sacré bleu," said Paul.

Things were purring along fairly smoothly when the Duke and Duchess of Windsor came in with two other couples.

"Uh, oh," said Maggie. "We won't see a waiter for the rest of the evening."

"Bon dieu," said Paul. (You may have guessed that he's French.)

The regal entourage was escorted to the table next to us. The Duchess sat at one end with the two men. The Duke sat at the other end with the two women. The show began.

"I'd like some more butter," said Maggie.

"Fat chance," said Paul with a heavy accent.

The Duchess held her two male companions enthralled, squealing with laughter and bouncing up and down like someone on a pogo stick. The two women *tried* to entertain the Duke, but he simply looked pained and distant. Every so often he allowed a thin smile to hover about his lips. The dialogue, which we could hear quite clearly, was defintely not vintage Noel Coward.

"Could I please have a menu?" called Maggie to the backs of the scurrying waiters.

"Ah, non," said Paul.

Edward Arnold looked miffed. The Duchess bounced higher. The Duke looked more and more aloof. We got hungrier and hungrier.

Our dinner finally arrived, and we fell upon it voraciously.

"The thing that burns me up," whispered Maggie, "is that they probably won't even get a check."

Paul mumbled another French epithet under his breath. Edward Arnold waved futilely for service.

Maggie was right. *No* check arrived for the royal table, but the entire staff gathered around to give them a fine send-off. The Duchess finally bounced to her feet with a few more squeals of laughter. The Duke rose expressionlessly—and pulled out a huge cigar, roughly the size of a salami. They all left in a cloud of blue smoke which Edward Arnold waved away with a grimace.

We received our check for an enormous sum, paid it and left. Marjorie and I had enjoyed the show tremendously.

"I never got my soup," muttered Maggie.

Paul said something unprintable even by French standards.

I mused to myself, she might have been my *mother*.

PAINTING LBJ

"**W**E want you to paint LBJ?" said the Voice from *Time*. The year was 1959.

"Who's LBJ," I asked.

"LBJ. You don't know who Lyndon Johnson is?"

"Oh, yes. Majority Leader. What's he done that's so important?"

"We expect big things from him."

"What does he look like?"

"Haggard. He used to be quite plump, but he recently had a massive heart attack, and now the flesh is hanging off him."

"Great! I'll do it. I love to paint dewlaps and wattles."

"He's very charming—at least in a crude sort of way."

"Doesn't he sometimes greet people when he's in the john?"

"That may . . . be a rumor. Anyway, *you* don't have to paint him *that* way.

"Okay, I'll do it as long as I don't have to paint him *that* way.

I decided to take the shuttle from Boston to New York—and from New York to Washington. While I was waiting for the plane in Boston, I realized that I had forgotten to bring my glasses. I don't wear them all the time, but I need them when I'm painting. I didn't have time to return to Orleans to get them. After a moment of panic, I remembered that my optician in New York had my prescription. I called him from Logan Airport. "No problem," he said. It would only take him an hour to make me a new pair. I could pick them up on my way through New York. I took the shuttle to Idlewild (now Kennedy), grabbed a cab into the city, picked up my new glasses, rushed back to the airport, and caught the next shuttle to D.C. Ah, modern technology!

"LBJ will sit for you as often and as long as you like," said the Washington bureau chief.

And if I clap, Tinkerbell will come back to life, I said to myself. "One thing," I asked, "Could he pose in daylight?"

"No problem."

"And I want a photographer with me—just in case."

"You don't need it, but if that's what you want, that's what you'll get. LBJ's a very charming guy. A little crude . . . but charming."

The next morning I met the photographer. Bourbon and mouthwash vied for supremacy on his breath.

"I'm the fastest man in the business," he boasted.

"But the other cover artists say that you don't get the pictures in focus," I said, turning away.

"Yes, I've heard they hate me."

"They don't hate you. They just wish you'd get the pictures in focus."

"Same thing," he said shakily.

"When is our appointment?"

"Just after lunch."

"And what time is sundown?"

"Don't be cynical."

The photographer (whom we'll call Herb) and I reported to the Great Man's office. LBJ shook our hands with much warmth in a firm double handclasp. Then he told us to wait, and he went back into his office. A steady stream of constituents came and went. The sun moved lower outside the window. I asked if I could make some notes concerning his coloration. The receptionist passed us some ball point pens with Johnson's photograph on them.

"Hey," said Herb. "That's one of my pictures. I'm not getting credit on the pen. Also I'm not getting any royalties."

As the hours passed, we stared gloomily at the portrait of LBJ above the receptionist's desk. It was a huge color photograph. Our subject was—well, rubicund. A living Norman Rockwell painting, plump and jolly. It had obviously been taken before his heart attack.

"That's the way my boss wants to be portrayed," said the receptionist proudly, as the sun moved lower over her shoulder.

More constitutents came and went. We noticed the double handclasp.

"He only gives *that* one to the people he thinks are important," said the secretary.

"Are *we* important?" I asked. "We got the double handclasp, but he still didn't pay you for using your photograph."

"Politians never *do*." finished Herb.

Herb and I picked up some literature from the table.

"More of my photographs," sighed Herb, "*without* credit—and *without* pay."

"But you did get the double handclasp," I said philosophically.

The sun neared the horizon, throwing long shadows across the cherubic Kodachrome portrait. LBJ paused from the day's occupation.

"I'm sorry to keep you waiting," he chuckled, "It won't be much longer now."

Two dozen elderly ladies entered, receiving the double clasp, a souvenir pen, and a kiss on the cheek.

"There's a bar nearby," whispered Herb.

"No, the sun's almost down."

"Don't worry. I have lights and reflectors. I'm *very* fast."

"I can pose now," said LBJ finally, as his secretary turned on the lights. Herb unpacked his equipment. I got out my things. LBJ headed into the bathroom.

Oh, no, I thought.

"Don't worry," said the secretary, "He's only shaving."

We could indeed hear the cheerful sound of an electric razor.

"He *is* posing out here?" whispered Herb.

"Yes, yes, those other stories are—exaggerated," said the secretary, as her boss re-entered the lighted room. He looked a bit green about the gills.

"Why is that?" I mumbled to Herb.

"My lights have a lot of yellow," said Herb.

"I think he used a green aftershave lotion," said the secretary.

"He looks like a *Munchkin*!" I groaned sotto voce to Herb, who was busy dodging about the room, snapping blurred photographs.

"You know," said LBJ, his dewlaps quivering angrily "no artist—or photographer has ever done me justice. See, look," he said, opening a drawer and handing us some newspaper clippings.

"Please sit still," I pleaded.

"Don't make me look skinny and weak," he said, shaking his wattles.

"Could you please pull down the blinds? The purple sunset is ruining the green facial hues," I suggested.

The Marjority Leader handed out some more newspaper clippings.

"Here's another one of mine," said Herb.

"You took *this*?" asked LBJ, giving Herb a hard look.

"Time's up," said the secretary, looking at her date book.

"But we only had twenty minutes," I said.

Herb clicked frantically, hopping unevenly about the desk.

"Unfortunately I can't pose again for about two weeks," said LBJ.

"My deadline is in *ten* days," I said.

"You'll think of something. Remember, *that's* the way I want to look," said LBJ, pointing to the blown up photograph.

"He was *charming*, wasn't he?" asked the *Time* editor back in New York.

"Sort of," I mumbled.

"He looks a little green, though," said the editor looking at Herb's color photographs.

"I'll fix that," I said hurriedly.

My haggard, but accurate portrait appeared on the newsstands. In those days *Time's* policy was to give the cover portrait to the sitter, if he or she asked for it. I knew LBJ didn't like my cover, but he requested it anyway.

Maybe he wanted to use it as a dartboard.

FUN WITH DICK AND PAT

"WOULD you like to paint Dick Nixon?" asked the Voice from *Time*. This was 1958 and he was Vice President.

"Not really," I said, "He has such a dull face."

"Well, how about Christian Herter?" asked the voice.

"Sure. *He* has a really great face."

"You have no sense of historical perspective."

"But a great sense of form and content," I replied.

I painted Herter.

A few years passed. Once again I heard my favorite voice.

"Well, you didn't want Dick. How would you like to do Pat?"

"Now you're talking. She has fascinating bone structure."

"O.K., get down to Washington as soon as you can. She's all set to pose."

I settled into the $350 a day suite at the Washington Sheraton and planned my schedule. I was on an expense account, of course. $2.50 for breakfast, $4.50 for lunch, and $14.50 for dinner. Tipping was a separate item. Well, for 1961, that wasn't *too* bad. I went down to *Time* headquarters where I overheard the bureau chief on the phone.

"We're sending our very best artist to paint Mrs. Nixon," he was saying, as he hung up.

"When do I start," I asked modestly.

"Eleven o'clock tomorrow morning. Here's the address."

"I looked at his note. "You mean the Vice President doesn't have an official residence?"

"Not yet," he said, "but they're working on it. It's not a big house, but they have a fair number of servants. Pat likes to run a tight ship.''

"What's she like? She looks a little . . . formidable.''

"Oh, no. With the press she's just about the most popular woman in Washington. They've nicknamed her 'The Skull', but it's an affectionate nickname. Her high cheekbones, you know. I think you'll like her.''

Next morning I got a cab and gave the Spring Valley address.

"Oh, you're visiting the Nixons,'' said the driver.

"I thought that address was a secret,'' I said.

The driver chuckled as he let me off in front of a house similar to the one that Snap, Crackle and Pop, the Rice Crispies elves, used to live in.

"Aren't there any guards or anything?'' I asked.

The driver shook his head philosophically and drove off. I rang the doorbell, gripping my easel, paint box, and carton of eggs. Pat answered the door. She was very gracious and *much* more attractive than her photographs. No servants were in evidence as she showed me around the compact house. All the furniture and paintings, it turned out, had been given by constituents and "friends''.

I began to set up my equipment, separating the egg yolks from the whites and mixing them with water.

"Save the whites,'' she said horified, "We can always use them.''

"Does your *cook* like that sort of thing?''

"Cook?'' She smiled thinly.

We set to work. I tried not to accentuate the cheekbones. After a while I noticed a trampoline outside the window.

"We just got that,'' said Pat, "Dick and the kids love to bounce around on it.''

I painted some more, wondering where those egg whites would end up. Julie and Tricia came in.

"Mommie's prettier than *that*,'' said Julie sternly.

"There's nothing to do,'' said Tricia, as they went into the servantless kitchen.

I worked some more on those famous cheekbones.

"What's for lunch?'' asked the children.

"Whatever you want,'' said Pat, the patient mother.

"Where's the cook?'' called Julie.

"Mommie's *very* busy,'' called Pat. "This is for a cover on *Time*.''

"What's at the movies?'' asked Tricia.

"Please hold still,'' I said.

"You know how children are,'' sighed Pat.

"Yes, I have four," I replied.

"I notice you keep looking at that trampoline," said Pat, "Would you like to give it a try? My husband likes it."

Images of Dick bouncing into the air clouded my vision momentarily.

"Mommie, can we go to the movies?" asked Tricia.

"Now you're making Mommie prettier," said Julie.

"Not now," said Pat. "Mommie is posing for *Time*."

"What's *Time*?" asked Julie.

"Mommie, please can't we go to the movies?" asked Tricia.

"No, no, *no*," cried Pat, like every harrassed mother in the world.

"Try to keep your cheekbones still," I cautioned.

The children came in once more and asked the same question in a loud chorus.

"Yes, yes," said Pat, "All right. *Go* to the movies."

"How many times in ages o'er," I said to myself, misquoting Shakespeare.

Pat gnashed her teeth.

"Sit up a little," I added cheerfully.

In the kitchen, I heard the sounds of rattling newspapers. The children came back.

"Mommie, there's *nothing* we want to see," they announced in unison.

"We can call it a day," I said.

"My husband will be home soon," said Pat. "Perhaps you could try out the trampoline together."

"I have to get going," I said, emptying my egg yolk down the sink.

"Goodbye," sang out Julie and Tricia as I left.

I checked in at *Time*.

"We're sending our very best artist to paint the Congressman," I overheard. "Yes, our very best artist—Henry Koerner."

"How did it go?" he asked, hanging up.

"Sort of like at home with Ozzie and Harriet," I said, crestfallen.

As I flew back to New York later I realized that for the rest of my life I'd be haunted by the fact that I had passed up the chance to see Richard Nixon bouncing around on a trampoline.

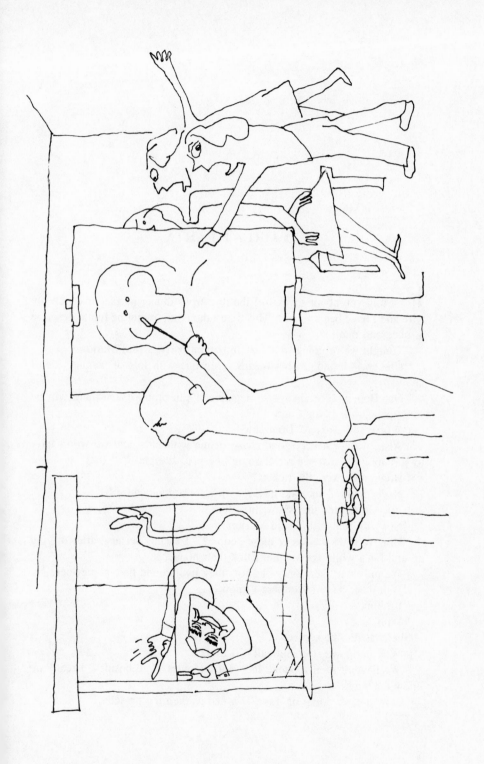

A GREAT PARTY

I've told you about several of the disastrous dinner parties to which my wife and I have been invited. This time I thought it might be fun to describe a successful one.

"Tonight we're going to a *very* important party," said Marjorie.

"Uh, oh," I said. "That means a big one with lots of people I don't know."

"Oh, Bob, you're always so negative. I can promise you there will be some people there you know."

"Worse and worse," I mumbled.

"Also, it's for a very good cause (name withheld), and we won't have to stay long because we're all going to a play at eight."

"How much were the tickets?"

"Never mind," she said hastily. "It's for a good cause."

"But we've seen that show three times."

"Not with this cast," said Marjorie.

"How well do we know these people?" I asked, because after driving around for a while, we couldn't find their house.

"We only met them once. I know they live around here somewhere."

"Will there be *anyone* there I know?"

"I thiiink so,."

"Who?"

She changed the subject.

"Why don't we stop and call?" I asked.

"We haven't seen a phone in twenty minutes. And besides, I really *do* know the way."

"How are we doing on gas?" I asked as the time passed.

Just then she shouted triumphantly, "There it is!", thus breaking off this friendly exchange.

"Oh my God, it's formal," I muttered as we spotted the other partygoers entering the house.

"We don't have time to go home and change," said Marjorie. "We'll just have to tell them we didn't know."

We entered sheepishly at the end of the line of regally-clad celebrants. Marjorie explained our predicament to our friendly host and hostess. They laughed and waved us in. Marjorie, of course, knew several people. I knew *no one*. My worst nightmare was coming true, and to add to my misery, every man there seemed to be a banker.

Our host held up his hands for silence and announced that we'd have to start dinner soon so we all could get to the theater on time.

Liveried servants began to bring food and drink to us as we sat around their spacious livingroom. The white wine was the best I had ever tasted. The food was good, too. Things were looking up. I asked what the wine was, since the bottle was carefully wrapped in a napkin.

"It's a secret. You have to guess," said our genial host.

Several of the bankers attempted small talk, but we could find no common ground. They asked me whether I painted portraits or landscapes—the only two categories of painting which they recognized.

"Mostly I paint nuns and bicycles," I said.

"I knew another artist once," said one of the bankers. "He was making a very good living selling his works for about a hundred dollars. Then he became very conceited and went hogwild, asking as much as three hundred dollars for a single picture. Imagine that. Three hundred dollars."

We started to discuss tennis.

"Most of these indoor tennis clubs are in bad financial shape," said one of the bankers.

I mentioned the time that I went to my favorite club and found that the local finance company had repossessed the nets.

"Ah, yes," said one of the bankers. "They had taken away the *net* assets."

Well, I thought, at least that was a beginning.

More great food and wine were served.

"We just love your paintings," said one of the tactful wives.

Now things were definitely looking up, and we even found we had some friends and interests in common. I tried to josh our host and hostess into telling me the name of the wine, but got nowhere. We all discussed the upcoming show, and there seemed to be some disagreement as to its nature.

"What *is* this wine?" asked a tennis-playing banker.

"You'll find out just before you leave," said our host.

I tried to pull the label-hiding napkin from a passing bottle. I was politely, but firmly, rebuffed.

Just as the festivities were reaching a climax, Marjorie approached me cautiously, waited for the proper moment, and whispered in my ear, "We're at the wrong party?"

In a flurry of embarrassment, Marjorie and I left as our host and hostess wished us well, toasting us with the unknown wine. All the other guests gave us a big hand.

We finally found the correct party two blocks away. The food was identical, because our second hosts had used the same caterer.

But we never found out what that white wine was.

THAT TICK INGRID

I WAS rereading one of my favorite books last week, *That Quail Robert* by Margaret Stanger. It was a national bestseller many years ago, partially because of its quaint, rickety, oversweet style. It concerns a quail adopted by a couple in Orleans. This quaint little bird entirely dominated their family life. At one point they even considered *not* attending their child's wedding in England because they were afraid the quail would be upset if they left. Robert eventually turned out to be a female and started laying eggs around the house and kicking them under the furniture. The quail became quite spoiled and had temper tantrums when not the center of attention. The amusing climax came when Robert was so miffed during a dinner party that he/she marched to the middle of the table, jumped into the aspic and splattered the startled guests.

Robert now lies peacefully buried a few feet from our house. A small gravestone with two grieving quails marks the spot.

As I dozed fitfully over the book, I half-dreamed I was reading. . . . .

THAT TICK INGRID
by
Frances Kafka

Until June of 19—, I had no idea of the great changes about to take place in our heretofore placid life. My husband, Oscar and I were sitting peacefully on our porch enjoying the pleasant Cape Cod evening, when I noticed a lovely colored dot on his bare arm. It was a little tick.

I was about to treat it in the traditional way, but then I noticed something rather extraordinary about the tiny thing. It seemed to be holding its two front feet together in such a way that I almost thought . . . Well, hard as it was to believe, the sweet little insect seemed to be saying grace. Such sensitivity in one so small is rare indeed, and I told my husband Oscar not to move for fear of disturbing the pious visitor's meal. At first Oscar was in no mood to comply. But after I had a little talk with him, he decided that I was right.

From the dainty movements and table manners of our minature dinner guest, I was sure that she was a girl bug. Dear me, a tiny tick is a lovely thing! She was a handsome, rusty brown color with muted shadings and a pretty white design on her back . . . every inch a lady! I called the children out to see her, and after a brief lecture, they agreed on the merits of the petite pilgrim. Our dog, Ringo and our cat Bette, in spite of a slight initial bias, soon joined us in accepting our new guest as a member of the family.

We all felt privileged to share the life of this sweet little creature, whom we decided to call Ingrid because of a resemblance to a former wellknown cinema figure. Soon it became clear that Ingrid was bringing a new joy into our lives. She was growing now, and yet she never seemed to need feeding. Also, because of the nature of her diet, she required no housebreaking.

She was lonely, however, at mealtimes, and so we fixed her a small place setting at the table. My younger daughter Lulu donated some of her doll plates, and Ingrid perched on a napkin. We gave the dear little thing a miniature bowl of tomato juice which, alas, she never touched. At night, she slept under the arm of Lulu's "Real-life, True-flesh" plastic doll. In the daytime she wandered freely about the house. Her winning ways and sweet personality captured our hearts completely.

Ingrid was growing now. Her soft brown coloring gave way to a pale green, and her contours began to fill out. She was no longer the adorable but scrawny insect that we had taken to our hearts. She showed a real fondness for our little boy, Randy, and was quite put out when he started locking his door at night. She also seemed genuinely grieved when our dog, Ringo wasted away mysteriously and died. Her tiny heart was, it seems, big enough to love the whole world . . that is, with the exception of birds. A gull or sparrow flying overhead was enough to send her into a state of panic. The very sight of one would send her darting up the nearest pantleg or sleeve.

Soon Ingrid was quite famous on Cape Cod. People came from miles around to visit with her, and a famous poet wrote a long epic about her. It was entitled *A (Tic)k At(tac)ked My (Toe)*. This led to her eventually being featured on the cover of *Time*. The Peking periodicals picked up the story and headlined it *American Insect Thrives While The People Die*. All of this notoriety, however, did not change Ingrid's sweet, simple disposition and loving nature.

Ingrid was now about the size and color of a large seedless grape. Her coat was heavier and richer; beautiful little specks of purple appeared along her spine. She didn't like to be left alone, and she wasn't happy at the beach or in the movies. We tried getting a sitter for her when we went out in the evenings, but no matter how many girls we brought around, she would never accept any of them. She loved us so much that she wanted us with her at all times. We, in turn, felt that giving up our selfish pleasures was a small sacrifice for the happiness of our tiny friend.

Ingrid thrived on all the attention she was getting from her many admirers. She soon became such a versatile hostess that an invitation to her salon became one of the most desired items in the whole country. It was rumored that several of the people who turned down invitations to Jackie Onassis's parties had appeared later at Ingrid's gatherings. In time, because of all this activity, we had to build a new wing onto the house.

Both of our children had been stricken with a strange, gradual anemia, and Ingrid was extremely upset when they were removed to the hospital. She would not come out from under the arm of her doll for days.

One day when we came back from visiting the children, we found a bearded man waiting for us on the front porch. He announced that he was a world-famous entomologist. He then told us to prepare ourselves for a shock. He had, he said, been studying some photographs of Ingrid and had come to a startling conclusion. In short, Ingrid was a *boy*. In fact, he was an extremely virile one and must be provided with some female companionship immediately. My husband, Oscar, at my bidding, became incensed and said that where he came from, they had a name for a man that would provide that kind of companionship . . . or even suggest it. The two men scuffled briefly, and then the professor left.

Through this time of trial, however, Ingrid preserved her (Oh, dear, I mean "his") dignity. In spite of all the jeering and off-color remarks which followed this startling disclosure, he retained his quiet good nature. In the end his sweetness won the love of even his most extreme detractors.

Then tragedy struck. Ingrid fell ill. Telegrams poured in from all over the world. The valiant insect, who was now about the size of a football, lay in an oxygen tent while the world held its breath. Offers of blood poured in from far and wide. My husband, Oscar, wasting away from grief, swallowed his pride and sent a pleading letter to the world famous expert with whom he had scuffled. This nasty man replied with a repetition of his former unspeakable suggestion. It was with mixed feelings of shame and desperation that we decided to comply with this prescription. My husband Oscar's eyes streamed with tears of disgust, as he rolled up the legs of his trousers and set off into the tall grass with a magnifying glass.

After this, Ingrid recovered and continued on his climb to new heights of fame. Of course, he now required a separate house for himself, his servants, and his *harem*. We no longer saw much of him, and, I must say with some regret, that our beloved tick was becoming slightly spoiled. We missed the cheerful patter of his many little feet about the house. It was lonely. Our dog and cat had wasted away. Our children were in the hospital. Until recently, we had been feeling strangely weak ourselves. My husband, Oscar, of course, was very busy. He had to give up his former job since supplying Ingrid with female companionship was now taking up all of his time. In keeping with his new profession, his personality had changed somewhat. He was becoming a wee bit sadistic. He was also beginning to wear purple and orange striped shirts, polka dot neckties, and yellow shoes. He smoked vile smelling foreign cigarettes. He just was not himself anymore.

It was a happy day when we received an invitation to Ingrid's Christmas party. We didn't even mind being at the foot of the table, far from the many celebrities surrounding Ingrid. The lovely meal proceeded pleasantly until it became clear that the Secretary of State, who was seated at Ingrid's left, was receiving more than his share of attention from the many guests. Ingrid, who now resembled a large purple watermelon, fumed silently for awhile at this misdirected adulation. When he could stand it no longer, he jumped up, stamped to the middle of the table, and jumped into the gravy tureen. There, he began energetically to dance the Charleston, thus splattering the guests from one end of the table to the other. He then did a swan dive into the punch bowl and flutterkicked back and forth until everyone fled in dismay.

The end of our story is cloaked in mystery. His servants say that Mr. Ingrid retired to his room in a rage. There his many footsteps could be heard stamping back and forth for hours. Later that night, a loud explosion, somewhat like the sound of a bursting balloon, echoed through the many halls of the house. In the morning, the police broke down the door, and found the room in shambles. After wading across the floor, they found what seemed to be the remains of a gigantic ruptured beach ball.

After a slight altercation with the authorities, Ingrid was quietly buried in the Orleans Cemetery. Thousands of mourners came to his funeral. His grave is marked by a simple stone on which are carved two grieving ticks . . . . . and the words "Ingrid, Beloved Tick, We Miss Him So".

ME-O-MY-O IN OHIO

"**W**E want you to be our featured artist," said the voice from the Ohio State Fair. "A quarter of a million people will see your work."

I had to admit he had a point.

"Okay," I said. "It sounds like fun."

"You know, it's the biggest state fair in the country. Texans claims theirs is the biggest, but they cheat. They have a football stadium attached to the fairgrounds. If you come to the opening, we'll pay you $1000 and all expenses."

"I'll be there," I said.

This was the summer of 1977, and everyone warned me it would be very hot in Ohio. I went to our local emporium and asked for the coolest pair of trousers in the store. In my size, the only ones to fit this qualification featured a large red and black checkerboard pattern. But at least they were cool.

My wife decided she did not wish to miss this great cultural event. Then my daughter Carri got the urge. We all flew to Columbus and were soon settled in our motel.

Later in the day we went to visit the fair.

"Don't miss the Swine Pavillion," we were told. "It's the most popular place there."

"It sounds great," we all said.

The grounds were indeed huge, and there was a race track in the middle. Let Texas beat that! I went to the Art Pavilion where my paintings were beautifully displayed. I was pleased to see the large crowds. My name was plastered all over the place. The main flow of traffic was definitely strongest toward the Swine Pavillion, which was—indescribably impressive. Later we saw the five-legged cow and ate some Dumbo Ears, which were huge, flat pieces of fried dough. Each time we ate these delicacies, I had to get a receipt, so I could be reimbursed. Nobody trusts artists.

We also noticed that many children (and some adults) were walking "Invisible Dogs". These consisted of an empty collar attached to a leash which contained a flexible metal rod. When the proud owner of this device strolled along holding it in front of him, the entire apparatus bobbed up and down looking like . . . an invisible dog. We resisted the temptation to buy this delightful contraption, even on an expense account.

Next came the Sheep Pavilion where all the attractive creatures were bright yellow.

"Why the color?" we asked.

"It improves the quality of the wool. It's washed out just before the judging," we were told.

The Bovine Pavilion was midly interesting, but the Vegetable Pavilion was the most peaceful. We never saw a soul there. We hurried back to the crowds at the deservedly popular Swine Pavilion.

"You're on a TV talk show tomorrow," the Arts Director told me. "We want to raise the cultural level of the whole place. Check in at the racetrack at 10 a.m."

"We'll catch you on TV at the motel," said Marjorie and Carri.

"You won't be able to get Dumbo Ears," I said.

"At least we won't be tripping over invisible dogs." said Marjorie.

"I wonder if *Green Acres* is on TV in Ohio," mused Carri.

"Don't you dare," I snapped.

"Remember to discuss the intricacies of egg tempera," said the director.

As scheduled on the following day, I dutifully appeared at the racetrack and was escorted into what seemed to be a huge trailer full of sound equipment. The first person I bumped into was Virginia Mayo.

"She's appearing in the road company of *Forty Carats*," whispered one of her young assistants.

"Ah, yes," I commented after Miss Mayo had left the room. "The salvation of all beautiful actresses who are slightly beyond their prime."

"Shh, she might hear you," gasped the petrified young lady, turning ashen.

"Ars gratia artis," I mumbled.

The actress was to appear last (the place of honor) on the hour interview show. I was going to be an early participant. A stage hand showed me to my place in the line of interviewees. Remember, we were in the middle of the racetrack. The audience sat in the stands.

"Everyone watches this show," I was warned.

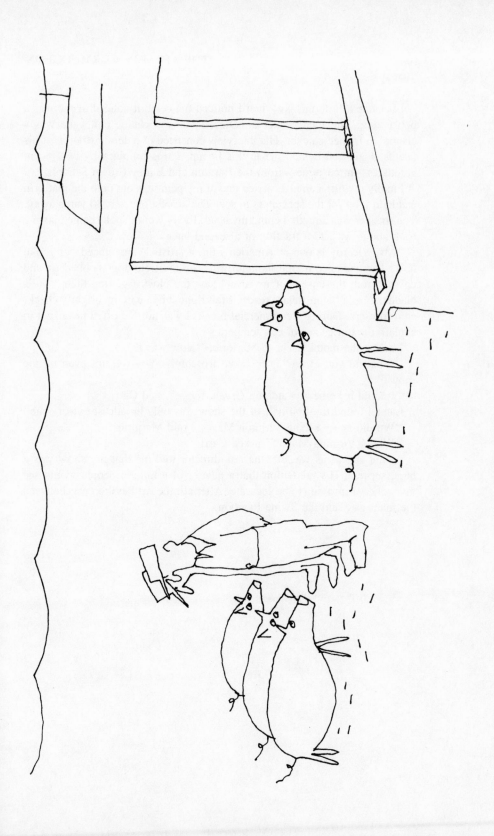

I became a little uneasy when I noticed the celebrity ahead of me was a police dog. The loudspeaker announced that my canine colleague was a champion frisbee-catcher. His interview consisted of a demonstration of his talents. I glanced behind me in this lineup. I was followed by two recent graduates—in costume—from the Barnum and Bailey Clown School.

Finally my turn came. I carried one of my paintings out onto the platform and held it up for the spectators to see. The nearest one was 30 yards away. The speaker was directly behind my head. Every word I spoke came blasting back about my ears a fraction of a second later.

"Mr. Viceroy is one of America's finest artists," announced our genial host. The audience roared its approval. The invisible dogs bobbed up and down. From the corner of my eye I saw the clowns getting their "pig's bladders" and "slapsticks" ready. I felt right at home in my brightly checkered trousers. During a commercial break, I was hurried off. I never got to explain the intricacies of egg tempera.

Back at the motel I said to Marjorie, "How was I?"

"What do you mean?" she asked irritably. "You weren't even *on* the show."

"I could have been watching *Green Acres*," said Carri.

Later I found the first half of the show was only broadcast out-of-state.

"We did enjoy seeing Virginia Mayo," said Marjorie.

"Who's Virginia Mayo?" asked Carri.

At the airport as we left, the arts director told me that my show was a huge success. His prediction that a quarter of a million people would see my work was proving to be accurate. After all, the Art Pavilion was between the main gate and the Swine Pavilion.

A FABULOUS FOURTH

Y EARS ago Orleans used to celebrate the Fourth of July with a display of fireworks at Nauset Beach. Taxpayers grumbled at the expense, but businessmen claimed that these festive explosions brought many new customers to the area, all with fistfuls of spending money. No matter what happened, everybody had a good time.

In expectation of the evening's events, really smart families would drive to the beach parking lot during the morning hours—in two cars, leaving one in a felicitous viewing position and returning home in the other, after sampling the excellent onion rings at the snack bar.

Others were not so smart. An hour before sunset, lines of automobiles (filled with saintly parents and grumpy children) formed a solid, bumper-touching line. Hikers called rude insults to the immobile drivers. Cyclists hurtling toward the beach drew shrill cries of rage from the latter.

"We have to go," Marjorie said to me and our four children. "It may be the last time"

"Can we take the dog?" asked Nicole.

Cocoa moaned at the mention of his name and crawled under the nearest sofa.

"Y-E-S," said Marjorie, who always spelled things in front of dogs and babies.

"I don't think his nibs wants to go," I said, carefully not mentioning the dog's name.

"He hates loud n-o-i-s-e-s," said Carri, following her mother's style.

"I really don't want to go," said Scott.

"You can have all the onion rings you want," I countered.

"Hurray," they all shouted. "We'll go."

"Mmm," groaned Cocoa from under the sofa.

101

"We better leave about two hours to get there," counseled Marjorie.

"You gotta be kidding," I said.

She wasn't.

As the sun neared the horizon, our roomy Ford station wagon was idling at a junction far from the beach.

"I'm thirsty," said Sean.

"You can have a drink—in an hour or so," I said.

Every few minutes we moved a few feet. Sean got out and ran around in circles with Cocoa on a leash.

"Get back in the car," I called. "I think we're about to move. And don't go too far away. The fog is rolling in. You may not be able to find us."

Our car moved a few yards.

"I think I see Brick Hill Road up ahead," said Marjorie, "Or maybe it's just a driveway.

"I'm thirsty," said Carri.

"We should have brought something to drink" I admitted, revving the engine to make sure it was still going.

"There's someone waving us into a field," I said.

"But we're twenty minutes away from the beach," said Scott.

"Twenty-five," I added.

We parked and started to walk.

"I can't see the road," said Carri.

"I can't see *you*," I said.

"We'd better walk holding hands. Are they really going to show the fireworks in the fog?" I asked.

"They *have* to," said Marjorie.

"Why can't they wait until tomorrow?" I asked.

"It just doesn't work that way," said Marjorie firmly, as we trudged along.

"We should have left Cocoa at home," said Scott. "The noises will scare him."

"He could hear the fireworks at home and he'd be twice as scared because he was alone," said Nicole, always the practical one.

"I see the parking lot up ahead," said Carri thirstily.

"No, that's another field," said Marjorie.

"Look, there's the booth," said Sean. "We must be there."

"Turn right and hope for the best," I said.

"There's a glow up ahead. It must be the snack bar," said Marjorie.

"Yes," I said, "You can tell by the long line."

"I want *two* orders of onion rings," said Scott. "I didn't even want to come."

"Get in line," I said.

"How can we tell when the fireworks go off?" asked Nicole.

"You'll hear the sound," I said.

"Are we still in line?" asked Carri.

"I thin-nk so," said Marjorie. "Hold out your hand and see if you touch someone."

"I just heard something," said Sean suddenly.

"There's a red glow over there," said Nicole.

"That's the light on a police car," I said.

"No, it's up in the sky," said Sean.

We heard the sound of explosions. Cocoa tried to bolt, but his leash restrained him.

"There's really a glow over there," said Nicole. "It's green, so it's not the police car."

"We'd better get a hamburger for Cocoa," said Sean. "He's going crazy."

More noises came from the sky.

"Get him two," I said.

"We only have about twenty people to go," said Nicole, who had been scouting up ahead.

"I see a pink glow over on the left," said Carri.

"That's probably the Windmill Lodge," I said.

"We'll have six, no *eight* orders of onion rings," I said as we reached the head of the line. "And two hamburgers for the dog."

"How do you want them?" asked the vendor.

"Does Cocoa like them rare or well done?" I asked.

"I don't know," said Nicole, "He's hiding under a table."

"One rare, one well done," I ordered.

"And two large Cokes for me," said Carri.

"Cocoa may be thirsty too," said Nicole.

"Okay, seven, no *nine* Cokes. One without a straw."

"I think I just heard something," said Marjorie, staring into the solid fog.

"How can we tell when they're all through?" said Scott.

"We'll hear a lot of noises all at once," said Marjorie.

"And, hopefully, a slight glow in the east," I said.

"Don't be sacrilegious," said Marjorie.

"The vendor named a monumental sum. "I don't have enough with me,"
I said in panic.

"It's all right," said Marjorie. "I have some."

"Not enough," I counted up.

"I have money, Dad," said Nicole.

"Which hamburger did Cocoa like the best?" asked Carri.

"I don't think he's eaten either one," said Scott dubiously, looking under
the table.

A loud series of noises came through the fog.

"I think that's the end," said Marjorie.

"I want another Coke," said Carri, looking at the blurred re-forming
line.

"Don't you dare," I said

"We might as well start back," said Scott glumly.

"We'll have to drag Cocoa," said Nicole.

"We can scatter a trail of hamburger pieces ahead of him," I suggested.

We started back up the hill to the field. After we reached our car, a
friendly policeman with a *very* strong flashlight guided us onto what we
guessed to be Nauset Beach Road. A long time later, we arrived home.
Cocoa bolted from the car.

"Do we have to do this next year?" queried Scott.

"Wasn't it fun?" said Marjorie.

"Yes," I said. "The best fireworks I ever heard."

NOTES FROM THE UNDERGROUND

T HE word is out. Now it's official. *It's been featured on TV.*

Noted *Time* critic, Robert Hughes, his locks blowing in his eyes, announced, "We only review the new." Later, he said, "We only ask, 'Is it new? Does it influence other people?' "

Whatever happened to "Is it any good?"

John Canaday in the *New York Times* had been warning us about this for a long time. He wrote that the cult of the new had replaced the cult of the worthy. Mr. Hughes and his fellow critics, for the last couple of decades, have fashioned the art world (*Art* in this article refers to the visual arts) with loving care, pruning out anything live and vital, treating with careful neglect work of which they disapprove.

Well, they got just what they wanted. Their vegetable garden is growing Birdseye Art: frozen, emotionless, flavorless. Now they say, "What went wrong? Why is the art of the last decade so disappointing?"

It seems to me that it all started in the '50s, which was a simpler and (except politically) more generous time. Abstract Expressionism was the fat cat, but all the kittens got cream. Conservative shows like the National Academy Annual were written up. Every artist's show was reviewed in the thin, austere art magazines. The realists were often panned, but at least they were recognized. Frederick Taubes even wrote letters to the critics asking them *not* to review his work, but they did anyway. Every Whitney Annual showed a roomful of realists. Thomas B. Hess, editor of *Art News*, didn't seem to like this. He had the theory that no art in all of history ever had merit if it was not *advanced*. Instead of looking for something he liked, he looked for something he *should* like.

Get it? "Is it new? Does it influence other people?"

When Hess became art critic for *New York*, he carried this theory to an extreme when he announced (with tongue-in-cheek coyness) that he had actually found a minor Italian Renaissance painter with Byzantine leanings, whose work showed *some* merit. He seemed to have forgotten about Botticelli, Bach, etc. At about the same time he was writing his book on Barnett Newman (surely one of the great retardataires) with his big closeups of Mondrians. Ad Reinhardt quipped, "He doesn't know his Hess from a hole in the ground."

At another time Hess praised de Kooning's technique of beating water into his oil paint, rhapsodizing that the subsequent works were thus born from a sort of "amniotic fluid". Of course, the offspring will have a short life.

In the '60's these views began to take hold. You see, once you believe that only the *new* has merit, you can turn off your critical faculties. All you have to do is *spot* the *new*.

Each critic and historian tried to discover his own trend. Pop Art (*Time* claims to have originated the term) was the only form of realism permitted. The objects shown must be cold and hard. The only emotion allowed was mild revulsion. The people portrayed must appear to be three days dead, with formaldehyde, not blood, in their veins.

Sculpture might be ordered over the telephone or produced from artists' blueprints in a factory. Many superstars no longer painted or sculpted. Like fashion designers, they prepared their fall collections. Some of these were lots of fun to hear about. Of course, I'm a little leery of art that is more fun to *hear* about than to see. I eavesdropped on the following conversation some years go:

A.   Did you see the new Oldenburg show?

B.   No. What's he doing this year?

C.   Well, he's making big toilets and sinks and things. Very funny . . . and listen to this. They're all *soft*! He's pointing out the ultimate uselessness of "practical" objects.

B.   He certainly is *clever*.

A.   Oh, then, you've seen them . . .

B.   Well, I haven't actually *seen* them . . .

Anyway in the '60's the magazines and newspapers stopped reviewing the conservative national shows. Art schools stopped teaching *life* drawing . . . or *any* drawing in some cases. Joseph Albers, when he became director of the Yale School of Fine Arts, after firing or humiliating into retirement the entire (and I repeat, entire) faculty, harangued his students with "If you don't do it my vay, I suggest you commit suicide." He was later described in the catalog of a retrospective as an understanding teacher who did not impose his own views on his pupils.

The Whitney Annual stopped showing anything but the *new* since Lloyd Goodrich no longer chose the show.

Finally, the art magazines decided to mention only a few favorites each month. At least, Taubes must have been happy. This neglect proved an unexpected bonanza to these publications, which eventually swelled to the size (and perhaps spirit) of *Vogue*. The unreviewed artists *had* to advertise, or no one would know they existed.

All non-pop realists have become, in fact, *non-people*. Some of the best-known and highest paid artists in the country are never mentioned in the *New York Times* or the art magazines. Thick dictionaries of living American artists now fail to list traditional realists.

John Canaday, before he resigned, pointed out that a few narrow-minded people were dominating the art world in this way. In his article *Wyeth That Menace* he said that if the work was good, it didn't matter if it was traditional. Shortly after this Canaday was no longer with the *New York Times*, which now uses words like "excrement" to refer to Wyeth's colors.

Traditionalists are presently in the same class as Kafka's hunger artist, whose talents were no longer appreciated. Sam Hunter, the well-known art historian, is reported to have said, "I like Adolph Gottlieb and I can't like both Adolph Gottlieb and Andrew Wyeth."

Why not? I think they're both good. Also notice that "can't."

I guess some reputations are safe, though. The great de Kooning refused, unlike most of his fellow Abstract Expressionists, to compromise and change his style in the last two decades. But wait. Here's what Kay Larson said recently in *New York*: "De Kooning is an important if not essential painter for the 1950s." Ouch! Later she accuses him of "false bravado" and says that some of his works "carry . . . self-congratulation to limits that would discomfit even a Sunday painter."

Look out, Willem. That amniotic fluid isn't *new* anymore.

Miss Larson recently made the important point that Lucas Samaras's "wit is psychological, where (Jasper) Johns's is epistemological."

Way to go, guys!

A Martian landing on earth and reading these publications would assume that almost all contemporary artists are making hard, cold, mechanical objects and figures, mostly derivative of early 20th century styles. Imagine if the same situation existed in other fields. Literary critics would not review Updike or Capote. They *would* review Burroughs (no? not Edgar Rice) and Warhol. Theater critics would not review Miller or Simon. They *would* review Beckett, Kaprow . . . and Warhol (or one of his look-a-likes). Movie critics would not review Coppola and Mikhailkov. They *would* review Brakhage, Isou and (of course) Warhol.

No, the *idea* has become more important than the art object. Finding obscure jokes and literary references has become the main goal of art criticism. For instance, Thomas B. Hess, in reviewing a show at the Whitney, was more interested in the fact that the melting ice from one piece of sculpture trickled over and wet the piece next to it. He spent a great deal of time musing upon whether the artist or the curator had planned this.

John Russell enjoys Jasper Johns's layers of reference in which the artist "seems to reinvent the notion of laughter . . . with his elemental cachinnations." I haven't seen too many people cachinnating over Johns's mild humor. Also, if risibility were the main criterion in evaluating art, imagine the fortune a drawing by *New Yorker* cartoonist George Prince would bring. How about "multi-layered difficulty . . . is the surest indication that important art is on the way?" I guess that means if it looks lousy, it's probably good. And, of course, if it looks good right off the bat, it's probably lousy. Another Russellism: "Realism, like the influenza, is always with us." What can the traditionalists do in the face of such "broadmindedness?" Perhaps a little elemental cachinnating of our own.

This would seen to sum up the view of the current art establishment, which is just as dictatorial as that of the Victorian Academics. Like Albers, they are saying to us non-persons, "If you don't do it my way, we think you should commit suicide."

I don't think we will.

MARTIN LUTHER KING REMEMBERED

" "W E want you to paint Martin Luther King," said the Voice from *Time*.

"Great," I said, "He's one of my heroes."

"Yes, well, anyway," said the Voice, picking up momentum, "He's going to be our 1964 'Man of the Year'. This doesn't mean that we agree with everything he's done. Remember, we had Adolph Hitler as 'Man of the Year'. We pass no judgement in these cases. We just tell it like it is. Actually, King may not be willing to pose. He doesn't like some of the things we've been saying about him. Anyway, if you're free, we'll pursue the idea and get back to you."

"Sounds good,"

"He doesn't want to pose," said the Voice a few days later. "We're going to break with tradition and tell him that he'll be 'Man of the Year' if he cooperates. Otherwise, the whole thing is off."

A day later the phone rang again.

"We told him that he would *not* be 'Man of the Year' if he didn't pose. He said 'I'll pose. I'll pose.' When can you get down to Birmingham?"

"Anytime you want. Can I take my wife?"

"It may be a little dangerous. Remember, Birmingham is a real hotbed. *You* may not be too safe yourself."

"I really want to go on this one," whispered Marjorie.

"We'll get back to you," said the Voice.

Marjorie called her parents, who tried to talk her out of going.

"Think of your poor orphaned children," they warned.

"Stay away from Birmingham," cautioned my father, "The Communists will get you."

"Don't worry," said the Voice a few days later, "King is in Atlanta.

We've got you a hotel suite. He'll pose as long as you want. Can we interview him while you paint?''

"I'd prefer it. He should have much more interesting expressions on his face that way. Can I . . ."

"Yes, yes, you can bring your wife," said the Voice.

Some friends in Atlanta insisted that we stay with them. However, we kept the hotel suite just for sittings. The Timeman and I waited for Dr. King to arrive.

"You know," said the Timeman, "A few years ago a negro wouldn't have been allowed above the ground floor of a hotel in Atlanta—except as a bellboy, of course."

The doorbell sounded. Dr. King and his assistant strode in, both dressed impeccably in charcoal grey suits, white shirts, and simple dark ties. I tucked in my bulging shirttails, and asked permission to remove my jacket.

"I'll keep mine on," said the Timeman.

I broke an egg, and we went to work. Dr. King outlined his early career with all its hardships, while I worried about his eyelids, which he held slightly closed, giving him an almost oriental look. He spoke in a careful, withdrawn manner. I began to paint his full cheeks, noting that he was putting on weight.

"How about some lunch?" asked the Timeman.

"I'll have a plain lettuce salad with garlic dressing, and a cup of tea. No cream. No sugar."

"I should go on a diet, too," I thought.

"Pastrami on rye and cheesecake," said the Timeman.

We munched away, some of us cheerfully. Dr. King's aide went into the bedroom to phone.

"Is he a bodyguard?" asked the Timeman.

"I don't have bodyguards," said Dr. King, "I sometimes have my aides with me, but I *never* have bodyguards. If someone wanted to get me, it would be a very simple matter."

He sipped his tea.

"A woman stabbed me once with a letter opener. The blade rested against the wall of my heart. The surgeons didn't dare remove it for several hours."

He put down his teacup.

"It was a *black* lady. She felt I wasn't militant enough."

He carefully wiped his mustache and suggested that we return to work. For the next hour he told careful, guarded stories.

"He doesn't trust us," said the Timeman afterward.

"Do you blame him?" I asked.

On the following day, Dr. King was a bit more relaxed. The Timeman asked about his finances. He carefully lidded his eyes.

"I draw a very small salary. My wife and I have one elderly car."

The Timeman started to interupt.

"Yes, you're going to say that I have an unlimited expense account. I have to travel great distances to do my work. I need a staff . . ."

"And bodyguards," added the Timeman.

"No," said Dr. King patiently. "I *don't* have bodyguards. I *do* have to have money to eat when I'm traveling."

"How about some lunch?" asked the Timeman.

"Plain lettuce, garlic dressing. And tea. No sugar. No cream," said Dr. King.

"I'll have the same," I said, tightening my belt.

"Cheeseburger, french fries, and Boston Cream Pie," said the Timeman.

"You know," said Dr. King, as he finished his Spartan repast, "the IRS audits me every year. They've never found anything. I think the FBI has me tapped. I get death threats all the time. But I know my cause is good."

A fine look came into his eyes, and I determined to capture it.

"Can I have your autograph, Dr. King?" asked the waiter.

Marjorie and a friend arrived at that point. They, of course, were quite anxious to meet Dr. King. He was gracious and relaxed, much more so than he was with members of the press.

On the third day the Timeman asked him about Gandhi.

"He is the inspirition for our whole movement. Without him we would not be able to accomplish anything."

The lunch break came. Everyone had the usual. After that we worked another hour or so and then called it quits. As we all shook hands, Dr. King said something like, "Thank you gentlemen. Please try to get it right."

"What did you think?" asked Marjorie later.

"Well," I said, "He was so careful and so noncommittal. He has to be, of course. *Time* hasn't always been kind to him. I hope the editors don't change this one around too much."

Later, I ran into the Timeman.

"Those boys upstairs *did* it again," he said, "They wrote it so that it seemed as if a *white* extremist stabbed King. The man was right not to trust us."

I agreed.

ABRAHAM LINCOLN

"**W**OULD you like to paint Abraham Lincoln?" asked the Voice from *Time*.

"Can we get him to sit still?" I countered.

"O.K., O.K.," said the Voice. "We'll send you every existing photograph."

"Do you want him with or without a beard?"

"Do whatever you want. Once the subject is dead, *Time* feels free to portray him . . ."

"Or her," I interjected, having been recently lectured on feminism by my wife.

"O.K., O.K. Him or her at any age," said the Voice. "You know we really wanted Henry Luce himself for this. The cover story is about rugged American individualism, but Henry demurred. He said we could put him on the cover when he died."

"But let's get back to Lincoln,"

"I guess Brady did it better than anybody."

"Yeah, but we want color."

"Was he pale or ruddy?" I asked. "And what color were his eyes?"

After a long pause, the Voice said, "Look, do it any want you want. Just make it good."

"How long have I got?"

"Six days. After all, God created the world in six days."

"Yes," I said. "But look at the world."

"You've been reading too much Samuel Beckett," said the Voice.

Anyway I came up with a portrait, part guesswork, part copy, and an entirely made-up right eye. After the cover appeared, at least three people inadvertently asked me if I had done it from a photograph. I thought this was quite humorous until I received a letter from a woman in West Virginia who told me that God was using the walls of her living room as a sort of private TV screen. The American Civil War was on that week, and I might, she said, be able to paint Lincoln from life.

"Dear Mr. Vickrey (she wrote), When you come down to sketch from my walls, you will find that the faces have an abstruse meaning for our age. The images are reproduced in this mysterious, recondite, inexplicable way. It has a great exoteric significance. (Good vocabulary, I thought. A bit weak on the spelling, though. Maybe I can find out about the color of his eyes.) I do not own a TV set, Mr. Vickrey. (At least she spells my name right.) I have seen some programs occasionally, but they paled into insignificance compared to my walls. It staggers one's equilibrium. (She's writing in "Timese" already.) I have been watching JFK, Mao Tse Tung, Roosevelt, Washington, Bird Phoenix, Trifon center, a beautiful young woman, Song of the Vowels. (Interesting progression, I mused.) My soul and mental facilities are tuned to such a keen degree, that I receive these images of Stupendous Grandeur, Portrature and Sublimity by Micro-radio waves. (How big are these walls?) As big as all Creation. (Hey, maybe she is psychic.) I'll list some of the things and faces which I had to leave off on account of the cost of getting out a pamphlet in 10,000 lots I took 500 to France. I wanted to get this out as quickly as possible. Can you give me the name of an agent or the agent that got out the King Edward and Mrs. Simpson story? I need some help in getting this out for world-wide benefit. (Oh, no, she's just looking for an agent, I sighed disappointedly. Ah, well. We're all human. I thought about suggesting she contact Maxwell Perkins when he showed up on her walls.) One last thing, however, before you make the long trip down here. I often invite people to look at these events of breath-taking, and unexpected profundity. But they claim not to see anything."

"I guess I'll never know the color of Honest Abe's eyes," I sighed.

I was all set to go to West Virginia, but something came up.

PAINTING BOBBY KENNEDY

In ancient Rome the politicians had an interesting approach to the never-ending battle between the liberals and the conservatives. One of *each* was elected, and they ruled on alternating days. This was supposed to achieve some sort of political balance, but actually (human nature being what it is) each consul would spend *his* day countermanding the pronouncements of his partner's previous day.

Such an archaic arrangement may seem impractical, but for many years *Time* was run in a similar manner.

The Editor-in-Chief (Henry Luce) was off in the clouds somewhere, visiting international dignitaries and shaping world policies. The managing editor passed judgement on everything that was printed, but seemed to have little to do with the day to day running of the publication. The two assistant managing editors, on the other hand, were concerned with the nitty gritty elements of getting out the magazine. These two (like the Roman consuls) took turns running things. One was a conservative Republican; the other was a liberal Democrat.

The results were—well, interesting. They shared an office, although each had a separate room. The secretary was usually an attractive lady of a nationality other than our own who answered the phone and polished her nails.

The two assistant managing editors were thus yoked together neck and neck, each striving for the position of managing editor. John P. Marquand carefully delineated such a contest in the banking world of *Point Of No Return*. The tacit agreement in such situations is that the one who is *not* promoted must resign. Naturally the political stand of the magazine on some issues veered back and forth at controlled intervals.

In 1964 I was commissioned to paint Bobby Kennedy. The Republican editor said to me, "We feel that Bobby is trying to steal Ken Keating's seat in the Senate, just the way the carpetbaggers did in the post-bellum South. We want you to paint him with a rather sick look on his face—like this." And he handed me a photograph in which Bobby *did* indeed look upon the verge of regurgitation. "In the background, we suggest a carpetbag."

"Fine," I said. "But I don't know what a carpetbag looks like."

"We'll send you one."

Working for *Time* is great, I said to myself.

"Auf wiedersehen," said the secretary as I left.

Shortly afterward the bag was delivered in the mail. It *was* truly magnificent: florid, intricate, vulgar. I could hardly wait to start painting it. A phone call came from the Republican editor, "Some of the people here don't like the idea of the carpetbag. Put it in anyway, but show it close up so you can't see what it is."

"What'll that prove?"

"*Some* people will get the point," he replied.

I went to work and painted the bag from a distance of five inches. Nobody to whom I showed the cover recognized the object. I went to deliver the painting, but I couldn't find the proper office. I asked directions from an intense office boy, who obviously hoped to ascend in the organization.

"Things are all changed around," he said. "The two editors wanted separate offices. *Corner* offices! Much more prestige that way. The whole floor has been torn up and everything has been redecorated."

"What happened to the people who used to be in the corner offices?"

"I gotta go now," he said quickly.

"But do the assistant managing editors have separate secretaries now?"

"Of course," he replied, pushing the "up" button of the elevator.

Twice as many fingernails to polish, I thought.

After Kafka-esque wandering, I found the proper office. It *was* magnificent.

"This ought to *really* do Bobby in," chortled the Republican editor, as he looked at my work.

"Your new place looks great," I said.

"Well, uh, thanks," he said modestly, looking out of the corner windows.

"So long," I said to his secretary as I left.

"Bon jour," she replied, not looking up from her nails.

Then the Democrat editor came on duty. "We can't have this sort of thing," he said. "We want a different kind of Bobby Kennedy cover. He should be attractive, firm, forthright, *in control*. Maybe with a mike in hand as he sways the crowds."

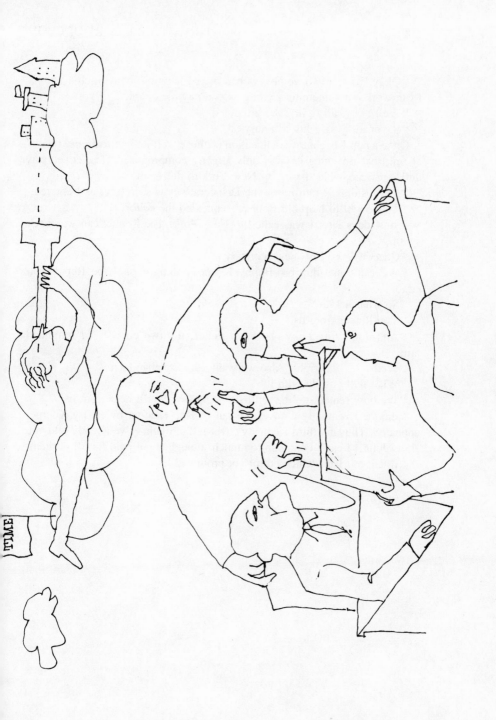

"Okay," I said. "I've always had mixed feelings about Bobby. I think I can work out something as long as you pay me double."

"Well . . . . all right," he grumbled.

"Sayonara," said his secretary.

Once again I began my delineation of those well-known features, rationalizing that my integrity was only *slightly* compromised. The cover was dull, but acceptable. I went to New York to deliver it.

"Buenos dias," murmured the Democrat's new secretary, as I entered.

"This ought to help old Bobby," chuckled the editor.

A few days later I was called to New York. The Republican was back again.

"Cheerio," said *his* new secretary.

"We can't use this pro-Bobby Kennedy thing," said the Republican editor.

"So what'll I do?"

"You'll hear from us."

"And don't forget my check, or rather, my two checks," I reminded him.

"Well . . . . all right. Also we want our carpetbag back."

"What will you do with it?

"We only rented it," he replied, "Anyway, you'll hear from us."

I didn't. Eventually a cover portrait of Ken Keating by Henry Koerner appeared. Thus my third Kennedy cover fell through. (I've already told you about John.) I can't complain too much, though. I got paid for all of them.

I'll tell you later which editor got promoted.

PAINTING JACKIE KENNEDY

"**J**ACKIE Kennedy is going to marry Aristotle Onassis," said the Voice from *Time*.

"Why?" I asked tactlessly.

"Well, uh, they say he's a good conversationalist," said the Voice. "Anyway, our messenger can be up there in Connecticut in two hours with a batch of photos. Can you have it ready by 11:00 a.m. tomorrow?"

"But this is Friday night. Thursday was always the deadline before."

"This is an emergency," continued the voice, "We'll put the finished portrait on a plane for Chicago in the morning. It'll be on the newsstands Monday."

"Which one do I paint?"

"Both,"

"In *one* night?"

"*You* can do it," said the Voice. "You did Moishe Dyan that fast,"

"Yeah, but he only had one eye."

"We'd use a photo, but we don't have one of them together. Anyway, call me after the messenger arrives," said the Voice. "You better take a nap for the next two hours."

I tried, but I couldn't get to sleep. I kept thinking back over my past adventures with the Kennedys. I painted John in 1959, but I failed to capture his charisma, and the cover was never printed. I designed the first 13-cent Kennedy airmail stamp. Everyone hated it (including myself). The government paid me, but didn't use it. I painted Bobby Kennedy—twice—but *Time*'s interoffice politics scratched both efforts.

"Here we go again," I sighed.

While waiting, my mind wandered to a dinner in Provincetown a few years before. Marjorie and I had to wait in the bar while our table was being prepared. I started to sit on a comfortable-looking cushion. "Stop," cried a nervous waiter, "Don't sit there—at least not right away. See that double indentation. It's, well, sort of sacred. Jackie Kennedy was sitting there a few seconds ago." We understood and moved elsewhere. The indentations remained sacrosanct—for at least fifteen minutes. Then, well, "sic transit Jackie."

The photos arrived, jolting me out of my reverie.

"They're all blurred and grainy," I said over the phone.

"Just make sure that Jackie is very beautiful. And don't have her wearing one of those funny little box-hats," pleaded the Voice from *Time*.

"But she's wearing one in every photo."

"Take if off," said the voice. "And, remember to put dark glasses on Ari."

"You've sent me more than a hundred pictures of him, and he's not wearing dark glasses in any of them."

I set to work. Marjorie went to bed at midnight. By 3:00 a.m., I had Jackie pretty well blocked in, and I began to think about Ari. As I said, there was no material that showed them together. I didn't know which one was taller. I tried to call the magazine, but nobody was there. So I *guessed* and made Ari taller—and I was *wrong*. Later, when people asked me about this, I always replied that they were standing on the stairs and that Ari was on the step behind Jackie.

Marjorie came down in the morning to fix Sean's breakfast. She looked long and hard. "Ari's glasses are good," she said tactfully.

"I don't like the damned thing either," I said.

"Who's the old guy with the young girl?" asked Sean (aged 12) as he left for school.

The messenger arrived promptly at 11:00 and took it (unfinished) from my hands. The Voice from *Time* was—careful, "We just sent it off to Chicago."

"I'm going to bed," I said.

Well, Monday it came out. It was my last (and possibly worst) *Time* cover to appear. I painted only one more after that: my President Humphrey portrait.

Postscript: A few years later my son attended a dance at the Kennedy compound in Hyannisport.

"Tell us. Tell us," Majorie and I said, "What is Jackie like?"

"Well," said Sean, "I guess she's attractive—for a middle-aged lady." Then he added, "I hope it won't hurt your feelings, Dad, but they're hanging your cover in the bathroom."

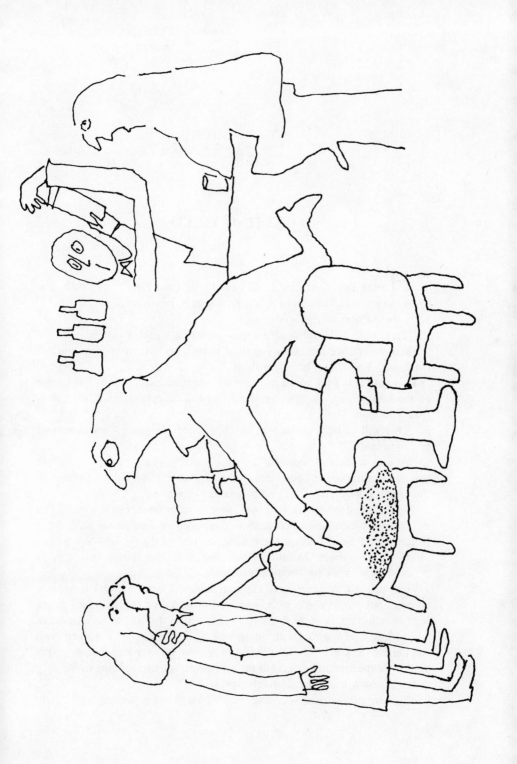

GETTING FIRED

"**H**ENRY Luce just died," said the Voice from *Time*. "We want you to do the memorial cover—From a photograph, of course."

"I should hope so," I said.

"Yes. Well, I'll send a messenger out with a batch of material. We've marked the one we like. Can you do it in one day? We want a drawing in black ink. You know, black for death."

Two hours later the messenger arrived. I called back, and we all agreed on the best photograph. The great man looked craggy, paternal, dignified. I went to work.

"This will leave a vacancy at the top," said Marjorie, "Someone will be promoted."

"And someone will be fired," I said. "Right now they have two assistant managing editors, one liberal and one conservative. One will be promoted. The other will quietly—seek employment elsewhere."

The liberal editor got the nod, and, sure enough, heads began to roll. The magazine masthead dwindled weekly. Conservative department heads were shifted out of New York and sent to far corners of the world—at a higher salary in some cases. Eventually *they* resigned. The conservative former editor went to work for Richard Nixon.

Time had always exercised vigorous editorial control over its literary content, but most people were surprised to hear that the magazine never tried to influence the style or content of its covers. In fact, the conservative editor once told me to go ahead and be as unflattering as I wanted with Republican subjects "because everyone knows we're a Republican magazine." Delineating the defects of the Democrats seemed to bring in the only criticism. Now things began to change.

The new editor, who was described by another publication as a "jolly owl-like man'', was determined to control the visual look of the magazine. Each artist was told exactly what to put in each cover—and what the proportions of each element should be. A cosmetic manufacturer was featured. The artist was told to "paint" the portrait using lipstick, rouge, and eyeliner pencil as his tools. He was dropped when he objected. Another artist was told to paint an airline tycoon on a piece of stainless steel "from the wing of one of his planes."

"How did it come out?" I asked.

"Just grey," he said. "I hope they use it before the paint falls off."

More artists were dropped.

"What will you do if he stops calling you," asked Marjorie.

"Celebrate," I said.

"I've got a great new idea," said the new editor excitedly when I next saw him. "We're thinking of eliminating the white band between the painting and the red border. How does that grab you?"

"The covers will look dirty," I said.

"Well, listen to this. Are you ready? We eliminate the *red border*."

"Then you'll look just like *Newsweek*."

He seemed crestfallen! "It was just an idea," he mumbled.

"The red border is famous all over the world. It makes *Time* a very good-looking magazine."

"We don't *want* a good-looking magazine. We want one that will stand out from all the others on the newsstand. The uglier the better."

"You're well on your way."

He continued, not hearing, "We want to use lots of poison-yellow diagonal bands. Also we're thinking of dividing the inside columns into little lined boxes."

"Then everything will look like obituaries."

"We may even put the headlines right across the faces."

"I gotta go," I said politely.

"Remember, lots of poison-yellow," he called after me.

I spoke to one of the other cover artists.

"They're paying some of the artists less now," he said, "Instead of calling the fast workers at the last minute, they commission six covers every week. The artist gets $2,000 if his painting is used. He gets $500 if it's *not* used."

"They must think artists are pretty dumb," I said, "Naturally each artist will work one quarter as hard."

"Also, they're dropping some of the older artists. One man supposedly went and cried. Artzybasheff is lucky.''

"Yeah, he's dead," I said.

"And they've cancelled all expense-paid trips.''

"Henry Koerner will be heartbroken. It'll ruin his whole life style.''

"What are you working on now?''

"A portrait of the North Korean leader.''

"Rots of ruck,'' he said.

A few days later I delivered the piece.

"The face is all right," said the editor, "But what's this big tiger in the background.''

"That's the symbol of North Korea. You said you wanted a tiger in the background.''

"But I wanted a *little* tiger. This one's bigger than the man's head.''

"The tiger's the best thing in the picture.''

"I agree, but I wanted a *little* tiger. Paint this one out and paint in a little tiger.''

"A big tiger will stand out more and the stripes are poison-yellow. It'll be the ugliest magazine on the newsstand,'' I said, throwing caution to the winds. I figured that either I was quitting or being fired.

His eyes narrowed. "I suppose you want more cover assignments," he said, misunderstanding.

"Fewer,'' I said.

"I guess you want to be *paid* more," he continued.

"No, I do them for fun, and it's no fun any more." I blundered on, "I like your politics and I like your books. But you have lousy visual taste.''

"What book did you like," he said, quite pleased.

"The one on J. D. Salinger.''

"Some of the other artists have been in to complain. We're not going to use *them* much any more,'' he said, still not believing that I did not wish to go on working under his terms. "Well, I'm glad we had this little talk. Now paint that big tiger out and paint in a little one.''

"Crop out the tiger if you want, but I won't change it.''

"That's an idea,'' he mused, sensing a way of saving both our faces, "Anyway, I'll get back to you.''

I told my artist friend about this discordant encounter.

"Nobody ever spoke to Henry like that before," he chuckled. "But then again, you're making more money than he is.''

"Except for his expense account,'' I sighed.

The editor called me a few days later. "We've decided to cancel the whole cover story," he said, "Come in next week. I want to talk to you.''

It turned out that suddenly I was Mr. Integrity. Nobody had ever stood up to this man before. And, of course, nobody had ever tried to quit *Time* before. It just wasn't done. For a year I was showered with more commissions than ever.

Then I was quietly dropped.

THE LAST SUPPER—

" "W e're inviting all the cover artists to a big party," said the secretary of the Voice from *Time*, "It's in San Francisco. Everyone else has accepted. It should be fun."

"But we've *all* been fired. Why should we come to this thing? Are they going to give us all solid gold watches?" I asked.

"Don't be upset. No one else is."

"*They* probably hope they'll get some more cover assignments."

"Well, some of them have said as much. Anyway," she drew a breath, "all expenses are paid. You—and your wife can come first class. It may be the last time. Henry is on an economy kick—at least for artists."

"All of us are pretty bitter," I said.

"Give it a try. We hope to see you." she finished.

"Let's do it," said Marjorie, "Your brother and my sister live just outside of San Francisco. The whole thing is ridiculous, but at least we'll get to see *them*."

"O.K.," I said.

In San Francisco we dressed up for the gala opening.

"See," said Marjorie. "They're treating us like royalty." We decended to the lobby. "I think our tumbrel has arrived," I said, hearing Time's magnificent limousine pull up.

"Wonderful to see—all of you artists," said the editor at the opening, "Chaliapin and Koerner are already here."

"You know," said Marjorie, "*they* don't look bitter."

"Chaliapin used to do more covers than all the rest of us put together. He looks pretty grim to me."

126

"Good to see you, uh, ...," said Chaliapin, forgetting my name and hurrying off.

"I don't like the new covers," said Marjorie cautiously, "But I think the editorial policy is much better."

"So do I," I said. "That's the irony."

"Roberto," said Koerner, hailing me, "Welcome to the 'Masque of the Red Death'."

"Good to see you," I said.

"Ah, yes," he said, looking around the room at the paintings. "The hanging of the has-beens. You know, I could paint a whole face in an hour and a half. Why, why are they doing this to us?"

"Henry wants the ugliest magazine on the newsstand. You should be flattered."

"Thank God Artzybasheff is dead," said Koerner, "This would have killed him."

"Could I interview you?" asked a young reporter. "We're looking for some sort of peg to hang this story on."

"Sure," I said, "Painting covers for *Time* has been a great experience."

"What do you mean, *has been*?" she asked.

"Bob, we have to go in to dinner," said Marjorie, pulling me away.

"Can I talk to you later?" asked the reporter.

"Yes, later," I called back.

"Don't you *dare*," whispered Marjorie.

We all had an excellent dinner, and then the speeches began. It seems that one by one the artists were being extravagantly praised. Each of us in turn was then asked to rise and be applauded, the ultimate humiliation. I caught Koerner's eye. I heard my name and bobbed slightly.

"Why didn't you stand up?" whispered Marjorie.

"See you later," pantomined the nearby reporter.

"Where were you—uh—Robert?" asked Chaliapin. "We didn't see you."

"Keep a low profile. Never give 'em a clear silhouette," I answered.

On our way out we ran into the conservative editor who had been edged out.

"What are you doing here?" I asked, "You look like the Ghost of Banquo."

Not answering, he looked glumly around the room at the latest cover artwork, "Well, Henry has finally got the magazine looking the way he wants it."

I agreed.

UPWARD AND ONWARD WITH THE KENNEDYS

W E'VE all been to the circus and seen the skit where a tiny car drives in—and dozens of clowns tumble out.

Something of this sort happened to my son Sean a few years ago. We gave him our old Toyota, and he decided to refashion it into the car of his dreams. He removed the back seat. Then he sawed a hole through the metal partition that separated the inside of the car from the trunk. This would allow him to take his friends to the drive-in without their paying. Such smuggling was quite common, and the drive-in employed a special guard with a flashlight who roamed the aisles with beady eyes watching for this sort of thing. Sean was determined to test the situation. He ushered his friends into the trunk, using a kind of logic. John, the largest, got in first, followed by Pygmy. Mike climbed in last. Sean with great difficulty closed the trunk and proceeded to the Wellfleet drive-in.

"One," said Sean innocently, as he approached the box office.

"Have a nice day," said the ticket seller mechanically.

"Thanks," came a muffled sound from the trunk.

"Shhh," said Sean as he drove hastily in. The show had already begun. Sean could tell because he could hear the soundtrack of the cartoon. Nothing was visible on the screen, since the sun was still up. Moans of distress began to compete with the soundtrack.

"Can we come out now?" whispered Pygmy.

"Not yet. The guard is three cars away. Shut up. You'll have to wait till it's dark."

"How can we tell in here?" moaned Mike.

Eventually the cartoon was over. Sean could just barely make out the end-titles.

"Oooh," came pitifully from the trunk.

128

The guard with the flashlight came suspiciously over and leaned against the car. He began to watch the film, as the sun finally set.

"Quiet," muttered Sean.

"Are you talking to me?" asked the guard, as he walked away.

Finally the film became visible.

"Okay," said Sean. "Come on through. Be careful, the guard is still around."

John pushed the back seat forward from the trunk and tried to squeeze through. "I can't make it," he groaned. "The hole's too small."

"Pull the seat back," said Sean. "Here he comes."

The guard passed once again flicking the beam of his flashlight against the trunk of the car.

"Next time," whispered Sean, "The smallest guy should get in *first*."

"Or saw a bigger hole," hissed John.

"Mmm," moaned Mike.

The people in the surrounding cars saw what was happening and began to enjoy this show better than the one on the screen.

"Maybe we could drive out, rearrange everybody, and come back," said Mike.

"Then we'd have to pay again," said Sean quite sensibly.

He pushed the seat back against the hole.

"Let's move to a different spot." mumbled John.

"That would just attract attention. Why don't you guys just shift around so that the smallest one is nearest the hole?"

Violent movements shook the little car. The spectators began to clap.

"I'm getting hungry," said Pygmy.

"And thirsty," said Mike from the stygian depths.

"I'll get you some food," said Sean. "What do you want?"

"A pizza—better make it small," said John.

"And a large Coke," said Bob

"Better make it three small Cokes," said Mike, "And some long straws. How about some popcorn? And candy bars."

"How do you want it," asked Sean. "Sort of like through a coal shute?"

"No, just toss it in to us like feeding chickens," snarled John. "And cancel the candy bars. They'd just melt in here."

Sean went to the snack bar and came back laden with goodies which he dutifully passed through the space. Munching and slurping sounds proceeded from the tiny Black Hole of Calcutta.

The second feature began and the guard went into his office.

"Okay now," said Sean.

He opened the trunk, and the occupants tumbled out like the people from Groucho's stateroom in *A Night At The Opera*. Cheers went up from all the nearby cars. The guard heard the sounds of jubilation and looked out—too late.

"After all this, the movie was lousy," said Sean when he told me about this many years later. I was intrigued by one of the details, though. After all, who else has had Bobby Kennedy's son locked in the trunk of a Toyota.

SOME OF MY FAVORITE BANKS

MOST people think of banks as formidable places where grim tellers deal with customers from behind iron bars while gimlet-eyed guards watch suspiciously. These institutions seem to be aware of this. For decades they've tried to change their image.

"You have a friend at ABC Trust," boomed one commercial years ago. Several others followed, each more friendly. Then the counterattack began: "You have a *banker* at XYZ." "No fooling around *here*" was the implication.

I remember the banks in the old Frank Capra movies. Sinister figures, usually portrayed by Lionel Barrymore, Edward Arnold, or Douglass Dumbrille were always threatening James Stewart, Gary Cooper, or Donna Reed. The little people, led by Regis Toomey or James Gleason, banded together and overcame these dark forces. Ah well!

My favorite banker was Frederic March in *The Best Years of Our Lives*. He approved loans based on *character*.

"Gosh darn it, these farmers need backing," he said. "So what if they don't own anything but their plows and their muscles. That's what this country is built on."

"We prefer collateral," muttered the directors.

Personally, I like going to the bank. The visit is so peaceful and relaxing. The customer enters to the sound of Muzak or Vivaldi's *Four Seasons*. Tasteful watercolors by a local artist adorn the walls. These works are suspended on plastic tubes descending from the ceiling, thus preserving the place from the desecration of nails and picture hangars. All office doors are open. "We have nothing to hide," they seem to say. No one at all like Lionel Barrymore is in evidence. All the little name plaques are informal. Everyone seems to be known by a nickname.

131

Sometime ago I went to my favorite local bank.

"I want to *lower* the debt limit on my Mastercard," I said.

"No one has ever asked that before," said the young lady, who looked a bit like Donna Reed. "Won't you reconsider?"

"No," I said. "My family seems to regard my debt limit as their allowance. Whatever it is, that's what they'll spend."

"Mmm," said the young lady dubiously.

Meanwhile, my faulty math caused me to be overdrawn. A tactful note arrived:

"OVERDRAFTS ARE CONTRARY TO SOUND BANKING PRACTICES."

A few months later, I blundered into the following situation.

"I have a strange request," I said to a young bank manager. "I'd like to photograph the hinges on your vault. It's for *Time*. They're doing a cover on Henry Clay Alexander, the president of the Morgan Bank. I need something interesting for the background. You have *great* hinges."

"I think I'd better talk to my superior," said the young man.

"What seems to be the problem?" asked this worthy gentleman a few minuters later.

He looked a bit like Edward Arnold. I explained my problem.

"Do you have any credentials?" asked Mr. Arnold.

"*Time* doesn't give credentials to artists," I said.

"Call us back in a couple of weeks," said Mr. Arnold.

"But you have the mortgage on my house, and I've had an account here for years. I'm not about to rob the place." I said.

"I'll have to look into it," he said firmly.

"Maybe you could use a portrait of J. P. Morgan," said the Voice fron *Time*. "Go down to Wall Street and check it out."

I did so.

"The portrait is hanging in the board room. Nobody is allowed to go in there except members of the board," said Douglass Dumbrille.

"How about the cleaning lady?" I asked.

He looked at the ceiling grimly.

"Remember this is for the cover of *Time*," I said.

"Well, maybe if *I* come with you," he said.

We entered the sacred premises. The large oil portrait was based on the famous Steichen photograph in which the highlight on the arm of the chair looked like a knife in the hand of the great man. Steichen had created one of the great metaphors for piratical enterprise. J.P. Morgan had no legal way of stopping him from reproducing this photographic portrait all over the world. Only, in this painted version, the highlight had been eliminated by the artist.

"Where's the knife?" I asked, referring to the famous story.

"I don't know what you're talking about," said Mr. Dumbrille, avoiding my eyes.

"Its one of the best-known stories of the century," I said.

"*I* never heard it," he said.

I started to climb on the board room table.

"You can't do that," he said.

"I just want to take a photograph of the portrait," I said, brandishing my Nikon.

"Nobody is allowed to walk on the table," he insisted. "Your shoes will scuff the surface."

"I'll take 'em off," I said, skidding to a stop in my socks.

Well, old J. P. didn't look right in the background of my *Time* cover.

"Go with the hinges," said the voice.

I went to visit most of the nearby vaults. Eventually I found one with the proper picturesque features and finished the cover.

"It's O.K.," said the voice. "Only Mr. Alexander looks as if he's about to rob his own bank."

"It's those glowering eyebrows," I said.

Soon I received another note from the local bank with the hinges.

"OVERDRAFTS ARE CONTRARY TO SOUND BANKING PRACTICES."

Sometime later, Marjorie and I moved permanently to Orleans. I tried to close my account in Connecticut.

"It would be easier if you kept a little something here," said the Connecticut banker.

"No," I said. "My mail will be cluttered up with bank statements."

"O.K.," he said gloomily.

I removed all my money (I thought) from this institution. For the next few years I received monthly statements to the effect that about 57 cents had accrued while the computers were closing my account. I was cheered by the fact that I was making approximately three cents per year in interest.

"You're sometimes overdrawn," said the banker in Orleans, who looked like James Stewart. "We'll balance your checkbook for you if you bring it in at the beginning of each month."

"What a great idea," I said enthusiastically.

A few months later the *bank* made a mistake in balancing my checkbook. Several checks bounced. I got another tactful notice about overdrafts. I went to see about it.

"Our fault," said Mr. Stewart cheerfully. "It won't happen again. By the way, we're now charging you $5 a month to balance your checkbook."

"Great bargain," I said.

Later I received a telephone call from one of the tellers.

"I think I gave you $10 too much," she said.

"I didn't count it. By the way, how did you figure out it was me?" I asked ungramatically.

"Just a guess," came the answer.

"I'm sure your memory is better than mine," I said. "What'll I do?"

"Just drop it off at your convenience," she said.

I received a note from the IRS, informing me they were putting a lien on my house for $12.93. They threatened to attach my bank account for this sum. I decided to discuss this problem downtown. I approached a new, very young teller.

"I want to find out how much I have in my account." I said.

"Name and account number please?" came the question from behind the plaque with the cheerful nickname.

I gave the information based on a check. She called the computer.

"You have no account here." she said.

Puffing myself up pompously I answered, "I had an account here before you were born."

"I'll get my superior," she said, looking at my paint spattered clothing.

A short while later, I was told the bank's computer had for years been carrying my account statistics under a number which was two digits off.

"Suppose the IRS had tried to attach my acount?" I asked.

"We would have told them you had no account here," was the answer.

It turned out I did *not* owe the IRS $12.93, but it *was* time for my quarterly tax installment so I sent in my check and left on a trip. When I returned, I found my check to the IRS would have bounced if the bank had not covered for me since a check from my agent had not cleared.

"We knew you were good for it," said the assistant manager.

"What a great bank!," I said.

In the following month of March, I decided to close out one of my accounts and transfer the money to another.

"I don't want those extra pennies knocking around," I said.

"Here's what you do," said Donna Reed. "Transfer all but five dollars

today. Then on the first of next month, come in, find out the exact amount in your account, and write a check transferring it."

"Let's see," I said. "That'll be April Fools' Day."

Eventually I was informed that I was $4500 overdrawn. I looked into it. A deposited check for $5000 had been recorded as $500 by the computer.

"There will be no penalty," said the voice from my favorite bank.

I thought of sending them a tactful note: "UNDERDRAFTS ARE CONTRARY TO SOUND ARTISTIC PRACTICES."

THE FINE ART OF BLUNDERING

Most people blunder once in awhile. I seem to do it quite often. Here's an example.

As an egg tempera painter, I work with pure powdered pigment ground in water and kept in jars—jars with metal tops. Sometimes the metal rusts and little particles fall into the pigment. To combat this, I tried putting pieces of cardboard, rubber or Kleenex under the caps. Nothing worked. Then I remembered seeing jelly jar caps with elastic edges. They used to come in many sizes. I wondered if I could find some such things today.

I went to several hardware stores. The houseware sections yielded nothing of the sort. In fact, the clerks recalled no such items. Finding this circular plastic object (1½ inches in diameter) with the elastic expandable edges presented a problem. Then an idea began to form in my fuddled brain . . .

Most men of my generation went through a certain ritual when we were young.

1. Wait till the drugstore is empty of customers.
2. Make sure the pharmacist on duty is a male.
3. Hint vaguely about the desired product.
4. Pretend to look at different items when other customers enter.
5. Perhaps buy a bottle of aspirin, a *National Geographic*, or some mouthwash until other customers leave.
6. After the druggist reaches under the counter and brings out the desired item (with a glance that sums up *The Old Testament, The Scarlet Letter*, and *Dante's Inferno*) skulk from the premises.

I approached the drugstore in Orleans where I have been a customer for more than 35 years. Entering furtively, I looked about for someone I knew. After all, I hadn't done this for several decades. Luckily, I spotted an old friend. I stood in line near her, waiting my turn and hoping that the other

137

customers would complete their transactions and leave. I waited, but they were not about to depart. I mumbled behind my hand to my friend that I would like to move to the far end of the counter. When we were safely out of earshot, I began my scenario, describing jelly jar caps. My friend looked blank.

"Well, this is a bit eccentric, but these caps look very much like—." And I named the object.

"Why, yes," she said, "I know what you mean." I quickly held up a little sample jar of blue paint which I had brought with me.

"Perhaps they would be under the counter," I said.

"No, no," she said cheerfully. "They're all out on the shelves now, right next to the door."

"Aren't you afraid of kids grabbing them and running out?"

"You're behind the times," she said heartily, striding toward the articles in question. "Let's see. You have lots to choose from."

Waiting for a browsing customer to pass by, I put down my jar of paint in an unobtrusive place. Just then, I noticed a prim lady with blue hair. She was looking at curlers nearby.

"What I would like to do," I said, "is buy a package of three. I want to try one on here and see if it fits."

The prim lady seemed frozen.

"If it does, I'll buy a package of a dozen. That's the approximate number of jars, I use."

"No," said my friend. "They only come in boxes of 12 now."

Still blundering ahead, I said, "I guess there's no point in trying one on here since I have to buy a dozen anyway."

"What kind do you want?" asked my friend as she pointed to the different brands. "And how about the ribbing?

"No," I said. "I don't think that will be necessary."

"Lubrication?" she said.

"No," I said. "That would mean that some greasy substance would get mixed up with all those egg yolks."

The prim lady just barely seemed to be coming back to life as I continued without thinking. "O.K., I'll take a package of 12 back to my studio and try them out. If they break, I guess I'll have to come back and get some more. I hope the mice don't get at them."

"I don't think mice would like latex," said my friend.

"Listen, the mice in my studio will eat *anything*. I hope they make these things stronger than they used to. After all, I have to put them on and take them off several times a day. And they have to last several months."

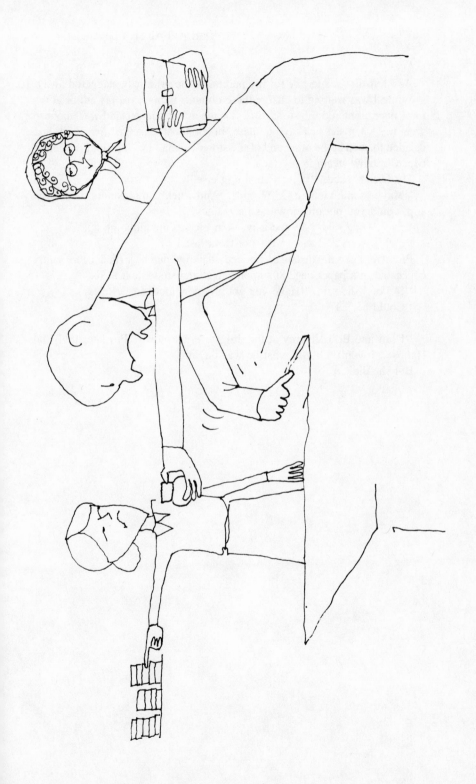

As I left the area to pay for my purchase, the prim lady staggered away.

While I was waiting to charge these dubious items, Pru, my editor at the local paper, entered the store. She saw me at the counter and was about to greet me when she saw my purchase, precipitously changed her mind, and decided to shop at the other end of the store. A small machine on the counter began to blow steam in my face.

My friend asked, "Is there anything else?"

"Maybe some vitamin C," I said, "And when you make out the charge slip, could you put this down as magazines?"

"Sure," she said, "by the way, your glasses are clouding up."

"Don't worry," I said, "It's not from lust."

Pru, from a safe distance, noticed that my purchase had been safely concealed in a paper bag. She approached and stood next to me.

"Hello," she said. "Have you got any new ideas for articles?"

"Could be," I said.

"I ran into Bob Vickrey at the drugstore just now," Pru later told Mal Hobbs. "I won't tell you what he was buying."

But she did!

LUNCH IN FLORIDA

Recently, I went to one of my favorite outdoor restaurants. I settled into place after shooing a few small lizards out of the way and ordering the Seafood Louie Salad. I pulled out the local paper. Soon a large crow flew down and began to bathe in the swimming pool nearby. Not wishing to interrupt his ablutions, I carefully put down my paper and watched. He washed himself very carefully, paying particular attention to the areas under his wings. Then he began to sample the water from various parts of the pool. He gargled several times and spat out the chlorine cocktail. Finally he made a shrill sound that seemed to indicate, "good–but not great" and flew off.

"Does this happen often?" I asked the waitress.

"Oh, yes," she said. "That's Jo-jo. He comes here every day at this time. Don't worry, he's cleaner than most of the people that swim here."

This was proven shortly afterward when a man returned from fishing in the Gulf and proceeded to wash off his gear by dunking it in the pool. "Come back little Jo-jo," I sighed.

My Salad Louie arrived as I finished reading the front page of the local paper. *Python Monty Is On The Loose In Naples* read the headline. "This escaped snake is *not* a lovable, zany British comedian," the owner was quoted as saying. "Also, he's not real fond of people. I guess he's probably curled up asleep in a bush somewhere in town."

Attractive little birds gathered about my feet to snatch up any tidbits that fell from the table. I dropped several extra pieces for them. This caused some larger birds to come sweeping out of the foliage and attack their smaller colleagues. The warfare became quite noisy, and eventually the smaller birds retired to the bushes, which were already quivering with life.

"Keep your eyes peeled for Monty," concluded the newspaper article.

I eased my chair away from the rustling undergrowth. A gull, sitting on a piling a few feet away, eyed the three baby shrimps in my salad. A few more lizards investigated my lunch and hurried off to a more tasty meal of flies and mosquitoes.

A hungry wasp settled on the lip of my bowl and looked over the giant smorgasbord. He hooked his toes over the edge and did a graceful swan dive into my lunch, flutter kicking through the Russian dressing and submerging under a leaf of bib lettuce. He didn't surface after several minutes, so I called the waitress over. In the style of Henny Youngman I announced, "There's a wasp in my salad."

"I don't see anything," she said.

"He's there just the same,"

"We prepare our food *very* carefully,"

"I know, I know," I said. "He just dove in about three minutes ago. There! Didn't you see that lettuce leaf move?"

"I'll get the head waiter," she said firmly, hurrying away. She returned shortly with a husky lad who was not about to take any guff from a middle-aged artist. I explained my predicament.

"I think you must be imagining it," he said, eyeing my two empty wine glasses and looking at me as if I were Don Birnham in *The Lost Weekend*.

"Okay," I said. "Reach in and see for yourself."

"No. *You* reach in and show me," he said, putting his clenched hands behind him.

"*I'm* not going to reach in," I said. "There. See. Another leaf moved."

"Where?" he asked, backing away into the quivering bushes. Behind him I thought I saw a snake move in the shadows—or was it the dappled sunlight on a root?

Just then the submerged marauder appeared from under a piece of crab meat and clambered up the side of the bowl, licking Russian dressing from his limbs and antennae. When he had partially cleaned himself up, he hurried groggily away.

As did I.

DINNER THEATER IN FLORIDA

"**H**AVE you ever been to a dinner theater?" asked Bill, my agent in Florida.

"Sure," I said. "You get your choice of chicken or steak, and you watch a one-set comedy with a cast of five. The audience chug-a-lugs before the play and during the intermission. If there *is* no intermission, the management puts one in. The lead is always an over-the-hill movie star. Who needs it?"

"No, no," said Bill, shaking his head sadly at my ignorance. "I mean a cast of 40 or 50, singing and dancing in huge production numbers, and the food is the best in town—at least on opening night. Even if it's a show you don't want to see, you have fun watching everyone sleep through it. We'll have to go next time you and Marjorie are here."

"Yes," we said, "Next time."

Well, next time rolled around, and we were pleasantly surprised to find that our friend, Beth Walsh, was in town, starring in *The Music Man*. We decided to go on opening night.

Marjorie and I, with Bill and his wife Barbara, arrived at the sacred portals and soon we were standing in line for our reserved tickets. Everyone seemed nervous and anxious to edge ahead of us.

"We have to eat by numbers," said Barbara.

"Sounds like West Point," I said.

"We're number 83," said Bill looking glumly at our card.

"How many tables are there?" I asked.

"About 100," he said.

"17, 18 and 19," boomed a voice over the loud speaker.

"And that's just for the salad course," said Barbara. "Why is that lady next to us bringing salad *and* dessert.?"

143

"She's cheating," said Bill. "She's afraid they'll run out of angel wings by the time her dessert number is called."

"The hearts of palm look good," I said wistfully, looking at her plate.

The four of us settled into our heavily cushioned red plush seats in front of a portrait of Victor Moore. Ethel and John Barrymore and 40 other well-known actors smiled ghoulishly at us from their ornate frames on the red velvet walls.

"They've all been painted from photographs by an old man in Spain who's never heard of any of these actors," said Bill.

"Drinks, anyone?" asked our elderly waitress, who was clad in black tights, with black mesh stockings, and one huge red garter. "It may be a while before they call your number."

"27, 28, 29," boomed the voice.

More numbers were announced for the hot entrées.

"Is there a separate call for the cold entrées?" asked Marjorie.

"There are no cold entrées," said Barbara. "Most of these people don't know what an entrée is. The word *hot* tips them off."

"Another round of drinks, folks? And perhaps another carafe of wine?" suggested our matronly waitress, snapping her garter.

"Yes, and could we have some bread to munch on?" we asked hungrily.

"That's part of your salad course," she said cheerfully.

"67, 68, 69!"

As the diners hurried down the ways, I seemed in my imagination to hear little bleating sounds coming from the flocks. And the gentleman out front looked a bit like a Judas goat.

"How about *another* round?" asked our gartered matron.

"I'd go to the ladies' room, but I'd miss my turn," said Barbara.

Our number finally was called, and we hurried down the red plush runway, steadying ourselves on the red plush railings. No interlopers with numbers like 86 or 87 were going to interpose themselves between us and our salads. The remains of several of these delicacies presented themselves to our eyes.

"More will be coming shortly," said a passing waitress. "Also, you'd better stock up on croissants. We're running low."

The hearts of palm were gone by the time I reached that section. I returned to our table, my two croissants awash in a sea of vinaigrette dressing.

"You should have gotten the bleu cheese," said Marjorie. "Then your croissant would stay dry."

I put them on my napkin to drain.

"The pipes in the ladies' room have burst," announced the loudspeaker, "everyone will have to use the men's room."

Finally our number was broadcast for the hot entrées.

"The chicken cordon bleu looks good," said Marjorie wistfully as the last piece was taken by someone ahead of us.

"Plenty more coming," said a passing voice.

Meanwhile we helped ourselves to filet mignon the size of poker chips. And eventually to some fresh chicken cordon bleu.

Barbara excused herself and went to the—men's room. She was relieved to find that the only occupant was a little old lady. Barbara was washing her hands when a slightly drunk man stumbled in.

"There are ladies here," called Barbara.

"Here, too," came a nervous voice from a stall.

"That's all right. I can do *this* with my eyes closed," said the man.

"Eat up, the show starts in three minutes," said Bill.

"Those angel wings were rather dull," I said, "I think I'll go back and get a cream puff."

"Show time," boomed the voice as the staff grabbed the remaining food and carried it from what became the stage.

"Another round, folks?" queried our Lady of the Garter once more. "You can drink during the show, but you can't order any more until the intermission."

"Quick, get to the other side of the table before someone gets those spaces," said Barbara. "Otherwise you'll have to watch the show over your shoulder."

The lights dimmed. The orchestra struck up the overture, and sure enough a cast of 50 talented singers and dancers began to perform. It may be prejudice, but we all thought our friend Beth Walsh was the best one in the show. The little boy in the part originated by Ron Howard was fine, too.

We noticed that many members of the elderly audience slept soundly during all the hullabaloo, but they woke up for another round of drinks at intermission. After the show, the cast mingled with the diners while we all sipped a glass of "complimentary" champagne. Everyone praised the talented young entertainers as they passed among us.

As we left I said to the youngest actor, "You were just as good as Ron Howard."

"Who's Ron Howard?" he asked.

A DUBIOUS DINNER

"THIS new restaurant is supposed to be very sophisticated," said Marjorie, "I'm really looking forward to it."

We drove for quite a while.

"I know it's around here somewhere," she said.

"What's so good about this place?" I asked.

"You'll see."

"Do I have to wear a tie?"

"I think it's required."

"O.K.," I sighed.

"There it *is*!" she said, "Up at the top of that hill."

"I'm not sure we'll get in," I commented, looking at the crowded parking lot.

"They don't take reservations,"

It was a three-story building, and all the upper lights were on. We walked in. The restaurant was deserted. Finally a swarthy man in a tuxedo came out.

"Yes," he said, eyeing us dubiously.

"Two," I said.

"Yes?" he said.

"For dinner," I added.

He led us to our table.

"Your—waitress will be with you presently," he said, looking at us very carefully.

While we waited, three men entered and hurried into the bar, where waitresses clad in tights greeted them.

"What kind of place did you say this was?" I asked.

"Shh," said Marjorie as several more men entered and went into the bar.

"You know, the bar doesn't look that big," I said.

"I think there's a back stairway somewhere," suggested Marjorie.

"I think this is a front for something or other," I whispered.

"Hi, folks," said our middle-aged waitress, adjusting her tights, and handing us our menus.

"We'll have a bottle of white wine," I suggested, "Do you have a wine list?"

"No, but I'll see what I can rustle up," she called over her shoulder.

She returned shortly and plunked a bottle of Dubonnet down on the table.

"I'll have the shrimp cocktail," said Marjorie.

"We're out of that," said the waitress.

"Marinated herring," I said.

"We're out of that, too."

"How about the clams casino?" asked Marjorie.

"Not tonight," said our waitress.

"What *do* you have?" I asked.

"I'll go see," she said, hurrying off.

"We have steak and lobster." She waved to some more men, who had just entered. "The lobster's frozen," she whispered.

"Two steaks, medium rare."

"Ketchup?"

"Do you have Béarnaise sauce?" asked Marjorie.

"What?" the waitress said, as there was a loud burst of laughter and applause from the miniscule bar. Some of the men peeked out at us.

"What kind of salad do we get?" asked Marjorie.

"Salad? I'll see." said our waitress cheerfully as she left.

"Don't worry," said Marjorie, patting my arm, "It'll be fine and. . . . . . ." She was drowned out by another burst of laughter. I sipped my Dubonnet.

"Funny," I said, "I see all these men come in, but I never see them leave."

"I guess there's a back door," said Marjorie. "Well, here's our dinner. The service is certainly good."

"I think they want to get us out of here fast," I said.

Just then another couple came in.

"See," said Marjorie, "Other people have heard about it."

While we were eating, our waitress hurried over.

"Choc or van?" she asked.

"We haven't finished yet." we said.

"Take your time, folks," she said, glancing at the other couple, who were leaving hurriedly.

"We'll skip dessert," I said.

"I have your check all ready." said our waitress quickly.

As Marjorie and I drove away, we noted that the parking lot was still full. The upstairs lights were blazing.

"I think they'll be good once they get on their feet," said Marjorie diplomatically.

"If the police don't shut them down," I mused, "Are you sure this is the place you read about?"

"Yes," said Marjorie, "But I guess it's under new management."

TENNIS WITH JUSTICE BLACK

T ENNIS these days is getting to be a very complicated game. Most of us now spend more time discussing our ailments than we do playing. Formerly the names on our lips were Ashe, Evert, Nastase and Connors. Now we talk of Diuril, Equagesic, Butazolidin and Extra-strength Tylenol.

Indeed, sometimes tennis looms importantly on the national political scene. A few years ago, I was commissioned by *Time* to paint Supreme Court Justice Hugo Black.

"Remember," said the Voice from *Time*, "He's in his eighties, and there's some pressure on him to retire. He's not cooperating and we're not sure he'll pose because he's afraid you'll make him look too old.

"So what should I do?" I asked.

"Make him look just the way he is," said the voice, "He used to be a member of the Ku Klux Klan and he's not happy about the possibility that this will be mentioned. His wife doesn't want him to pose either. She's afraid a portrait that makes him look too old will increase the pressure to retire."

Justice Black finally granted me one half-hearted sitting of indeterminate length. I asked if a reporter could interview him at the same time. He agreed with little enthusiasm. When I arrived at his office, he introduced me to his wife.

"She's going to watch," he said, eyeing me with suspicion.

This fine lady sat behind me while I worked. Every time I painted a wrinkle, she came out with a loud "tsk, tsk, tsk." Each dewlap brought forth a groan. Crow's feet caused incoherent mumbling. When I began to depict his handsome bald dome, I could see her cringe. When we took a break, she hurriedly pulled out a photograph of the Justice at about the age of 40. At that time, he had a full head of hair.

"This is the way I think of him," she said. "Why can't you paint him like this?" I noisily swirled my brush in my glass of egg yolk.

When the sitting resumed, Justice Black relaxed a bit and began to tell some of his great humorous stories. This added smile wrinkles to the corner of his mouth. "Tsk, tsk, tsk," clicked his wife behind me.

"Tell me about the Ku Klux Klan," said the *Time* reporter.

"Turn a little to the left," I pleaded.

"You know," he said, quickly changing the subject, "one of your editors has challenged me to tennis tomorrow. He's about forty years younger than I am."

"How does the KKK feel about your liberal positions now?" queried the reporter.

"On, no," groaned his wife from behind me as little wrinkles appeared between his brows.

"I hope I can play well," said Justice Black. "He's so much younger than I am."

"Don't move your head," I counseled. "Tsk, tsk," came again from behind me.

"I wonder if he's a good player," murmured Justice Black unhappily. "I'm not sure when I can pose again."

As the reporter and I left, we heard the great man mumble, "My backhand's a little rusty."

That night I had a long talk with the tennis-playing editor.

"How good are you?" I asked.

"Actually, I'm very good."

"Do you lose often?" I asked.

"Almost never," he said firmly.

"Well, look, if you lose tomorrow we'll have a real pussycat on our hands. If you win, the whole cover story may fall through."

"Mmm," he replied unhappily.

Anyway the match took place on the following morning and the *Time* man was "defeated" ignominiously. Justice Black was in rapture. He agreed to pose anytime and for as long as we wanted.

I wonder if Gorbachev plays tennis?

DINNER IN OZ

"**W**HAT do you want for your birthday?" I asked Marjorie sometime ago.

"Dinner at the best restaurant on Cape Cod?" she replied without blinking.

"Okay," I said after a slight hesitation. "Let's line up some other people and we'll have a party."

Actually Marjorie and I had been going to this restaurant off and on for more than 30 years, although the management had changed occasionally. The first time we visited this wonderful world of gourmet cuisine, we were a bit surprised by the service. A milkmaid straight from the court of Marie Antoinette seated us in our elegant surroundings. She wore a hoop skirt and lace bonnet. Our waiter appeared. He was dressed as a shepherd from a painting by Watteau, with lacy knickers, frilly cuffs—and a crook. (No, not one of the Corleone brothers). Luckily for him, he looked like an extremely beefy football player. We were relieved to notice that after his initial appearance, he put aside his crook. After all, we sheep were already safely under control.

I excused myself and went to seek out the men's room. Our hosts pointed to a busily papered wall. No opening was visible. I felt around for a while and finally located a disguised door.

"Is this for men or women?" I called out tactlessly.

Our two hosts smiled thinly. By trial and error, I located the room with the proper fixtures.

Our crookless shepherd served us a sumptuous meal . . . and a sumptuous check.

"That was great!" said Marjorie on the way home.
"We'll have to come here again . . . in a few years," I said.

After this allotted span, we decided that another visit to the sacred shrine was in order. We got some friends together for the pilgrimage. A different management had taken over. I was quite disappointed. Our milkmaid waitress no longer sported a hoop skirt and (even more disappointing) our waiter shepherd no longer carried a crook.
"What a wonder dinner!" said our friends.
"The sauce on the chicken and veal was identical," said Marjorie. "But don't you just love the ambience?"
I still couldn't find the men's room in the wallpaper.
More years passed. Marjorie and I were driving by the hallowed grounds when she said, "Let's see if they can take us on the spur of the moment. We're just in time for the early sitting, and it *is* off-season."
We asked our impeccable host if this was possible.
"I'll try to fit you in," he said. "Please wait in the gift shop."
We did . . . for an hour, looking at framed pages from Victorian magazines, priced at what would now be several hundred dollars. We did not purchase any of these fine objects. Finally our host announced that they couldn't take us.
"May I use the men's room?" I asked.
If you can find it, his glance seemed to say.

It was now 1984 and time for the birthday dinner. Marjorie and I asked our friends, Dick and Barbara, if they would like to join us. They expressed great enthusiasm. We also asked our friends, Paul and Martha.
"Sure," said Paul, adding facetiously, "We'll just give up our trip to Europe."
We journeyed to the Land of Oz and arrived at the Emerald City at 6:20 just making it under the deadline. As we entered the temple, I heard (perhaps in my imagination) the sound of chanting. And *was* that the smell of incense?
"No," said Marjorie, "That's thyme."
Our attractive and efficient waitress placed before us menus which teemed with columns of delicacies looking and sounding like exquisite French poetry. She then left to fill our drink orders. We asked our young busboy what some of the foreign phrases meant.
"You got me," he said.
"Would you like a translation?" asked our waitress when she returned.
We all nodded vigorously. The most intriguing dish she named consisted

of fricasseed snails. *That* I wanted to see, but no one (including myself) was willing to give it a try.

Our first course arrived: *Mousse de Trois Poissons*. It looked like a blue, turned-down-mouth. I turned the dish 180 degrees and now it looked like a broad smile. Someone else had fingers of lamb.

"I didn't know lamb had fingers," said Marjorie.

Then came the soup.

"My consommé is good," said Paul. "But it needs salt."

There was no salt on the table.

"It would be like asking for ketchup," I said.

Paul asked anyway. He received a salt shaker about the size of a large Chiclet.

"Salt isn't good for you," said Marjorie.

She and I had the pear and lemon soup. It was cold and sweet.

"It would be just perfect over ice cream," we agreed.

"The rolls are delicious," said Martha.

"If you eat them in the first three minutes." I said.

A fine salad arrived.

"I'll have mine after the main course," said Barbara.

The dish was efficiently whisked away.

"Let's see if you get it later," I whispered.

The *Sorbet du Jour* arrived. "To cleanse our palates."

"My God, it's unsweetened grapefruit," I said.

"That won't just cleanse our palates, it will scour them." said Paul.

Dick, tactfully, said nothing.

After consubstantiation or transubstantiation (I'm not sure which) the main course arrived.

"No, no," I said, looking at the delectable slices of red meat. "I ordered the duck."

"That *is* the duck," said our waitress firmly.

"I thought it was lamb, too," said Dick who was having the same dish.

"I seem to have sausage," said Martha.

"That's the lobster," said our waitress. "The sole is underneath."

Marjorie and Paul looked at their crimson viands and said, "We have the beef."

"Lamb," said our waitress.

I began to feel like Aaron Slick from Pun'kin Crick.

"This duck is great," I said. "Is it rare or raw?"

"It's singed," said our waitress, tapping her foot impatiently.

"How's your beef?" asked Barbara.

"I don't know," she said, "The spices in the sauce are overwhelming it."

"Pass the salt," said Paul.

"I can't finish all this . . . lamb," said Marjorie. "It's too rare. But everything else was just perfect."

"Don't ask for a doggie bag," I said. "Besides, we have to have our . . ." and I tried to pronounce the French name of the next course.

"Cookies and mints leading up to dessert," said our waitress.

All of the above proved to be excellent, except for the madeleines.

"If Proust had had a madeleine like this," said someone, "He'd never have written *Remembrance Of Things Past.*

"They *did* remember my salad," whispered Barbara.

The desserts arrived, each richer than the next. We all shared them.

"Luckily I took two Tums before we came," said Paul.

"This was a great theatrical experience," said Martha.

"I'm still hungry," I muttered.

The bill was placed on the table.

"We really *will* have to cancel our trip to Europe," said Paul.

"I knew I'd find some use for these fifty dollar bills," I said.

The secret entrance to the men's room remained unchanged.

Later that evening I felt a strange gnawing in my stomach, and while I munched on a slice of warmed-over-pizza, I said to myself, Oz is a great place to visit. But I wouldn't want to live there.

GUNFIGHT AT THE ORLEANS CORRAL

W E all remember those wonderful westerns where the heroic gunfighter confronted the bad guys and prevailed against all odds. Gary Cooper did it in *High Noon*. One by one, all his friends and deputies deserted him, until finally he was alone, face to face with destiny. In *A Fistful Of Dollars*, Clint Eastwood (the man with no name) rode into a small town, cleaned up its messy problems, and left. In several versions of the gunfight at the O.K. Corral, Wyatt Earp more or less singlehandedly eliminated the infamous Clanton gang. And let's not forget *Shane*, where our hero (Alan Ladd) confronted the cattle barons and did away with their evil influence. At the end of the film Brandon deWilde called after him, "Shane, Shane. Come back, Shane."

Most of us believe such things never happen in our mundane lives. I'm beginning to change my mind. Here's the story of my own gunfight.

Recently I was informed I could have a hearing with the Orleans Water Department. For three and a half years they never told me I had this right. In order to gather my forces, I approached my numerous water experts and advisors.

"I can't come," said the most important one, handing me a book called *Water Fit To Drink*. "There would be a conflict of interest."

"I'm not allowed to be there by law," said the water commissioner of another town.

"I don't live in Orleans," said a third.

"I agree with everything you're doing," said a fourth, "But my health is bad and I never go out."

"I'd be fired," said a fifth.

"It wouldn't be proper for me to come," said a sixth (the former Orleans

158

water superintendent). "However, we knew how acidic our water was over 20 years ago when we installed town water. We only put in iron pipes because we knew the acid would corrode anything made of copper."

"It would be pointless for me to come," said my lawyer. "Also, I'm doing something else that night. But I'll tell you exactly how to go about it. *Something* has to be done. The summer people all say the water is much worse this year."

Well, Gary Cooper, Clint Eastwood and Alan Ladd did it. So I prepared to face the big guns.

"You can't bring a tape recorder," said the clerk.

"Will the room be air conditioned?" I asked.

"No," was the answer.

"How come?" I asked with a touch of paranoia.

"We always turn it off at four o'clock," she said.

I relaxed.

"We'll have lots of water experts there," she added.

I grew tense.

"I hope *you're* going to be there," I later said glumly to a reporter from *The Cape Codder*. "I have to get some sort of statement from the commissioners. Also they've forbidden recording machines."

"I'm bringing mine anyway," he said. "They'll have to call the police and drag me from the building."

As an amateur gunfighter with a battered tote bag full of papers and spotted laundry, I went to face the commissioners, the superintendent, a doctor, a water engineer and other experts.

What am I doing here? I asked myself as I entered the room, which *did* look at bit like the O.K. Corral.

We were hemmed in on all sides by counters and desks from behind which the snipers could fire. Several people came to watch. The reporter arrived at one minute to seven, sat down, and placed a tape recorder firmly on the conference table. The first shot had been fired. The commissioners never blinked.

The meeting began. I stood, displaying my badly stained T-shirt and pulled out a pair of equally stained and tattered undershorts.

"This is why I'm called 'Old Iron Pants'." I announced. Then I read a mock funeral oration for Orleans water, based on Mark Antony's speech from Shakespeare's *Julius Caesar*. My voice was tense and strained. I plunged on.

"Their own publication tells us that water on Cape Cod tends to be acidic.

It also says, 'Iron in water in concentration of .3 ppm or greater may: give the water a bittersweet astringent taste, cause an unpleasant odor, often gives (sic) the water a brownish color and causes staining of laundry and porcelain.' Two Orleans sources seem to be at that level now. On March 14th the iron level at our house was .5 and by then most of our clothing and many of our fixtures had been ruined. But 'it poses no health hazard' say our friends. They are 'comfortable,' and they are honorable men.

"As acidic water corrodes copper plumbing all over town, we hundreds of uncomfortable ones read: 'Corrosiveness (of acidic water) may be the factor in water that accounts for increased cardio-vascular problems.' Corrosion of asbestos cement pipes by acidic water may even cause cancer. Our health department has released figures that show our acidic level to be worsening.

"If you have tears, prepare to shed them now. All of Cape groundwater may be in trouble. Russell Sylva of the Department of Environmental Quality Engineering says 'What I fear most is waking up to the news that we have lost the water on Cape Cod.' We 'have great vulnerability to acid rain damage,' says *The Boston Globe*. 'More serious than indicated earlier. Every part of the Northeast contains acid-dead water bodies.' Our Board of Health recently released figures that say two of the town wells are above the limits recommended by the Environmental Protection Agency for iron. Eight have acidic levels over these limits. But our commissioners are 'comfortable' and they are honorable men."

I could hear the doctor from the health department loading his weapon from behind the counter in back of me.

They've got me surrounded, I said to myself.

Then the fun began. Members of the audience made ringing speeches, much better than mine. Bang! The doctor behind me fired and failed to shake my facts. Riffling through my piles of evidence, I managed to come up with the proof of my statements. The commissioner on my right withdrew into total silence. The laconic commissioner at the end of the table prepared for his attack. He spoke with his excellent dry delivery. However, he misfired, tangled in the telephone wires of his own personal problems.

Whew! That was close, I thought, as we returned to the main questions at hand. The chairman seemed genuinely concerned and anxious finally to face up to the problems. My nervousness lifted somewhat. I heard movement from the sniper behind me. The good doctor dramatically pulled from his holster a container of the spot remover WHINK carefully wrapped in a baggie. "Since you love this product so much, I've brought you a bottle. I wouldn't let my hands touch it," he said, reading a list of its contents.

I ducked, receiving a flesh wound, and returned fire.

"I'll never use it again."

He then questioned me about some of my medical facts. I tried to hand him a xeroxed page from the book *Water Fit to Drink*. Zing came the shot: "Unless it's written by a doctor, I refuse to let my hands touch it. And what's this stuff about asbestos cement pipe possibly causing cancer?"

"That's one problem we don't have to worry about," announced the chairman.

"Wait a minute," said the laconic connissioner, "There's one stretch of pipe that might be."

Kapow! I ducked, finding an unexpected confirmation. The silent commissioner became more silent. Fire from the spectators grew intense. One eloquent lady was waving a green-stained bowl over her head. The reporter put a new tape into his machine, much to the laconic commissioner's annoyance. The clerk seemed to be enjoying the whole thing from the other side of the corral.

"I never heard of your problem until a little while ago," the chairman said.

"In other words," I said, "The clerk is supposed to stall the complainers with a vague excuse and a free bottle of Rover Rust Remover."

"Is that what you give them?" asked the chairman.

"No, no, it's—wait a minute—it *is* Rover Rust Remover," said the clerk holding up a bottle.

"With a little circle over the 'Rover'," I said.

"You're right," she said.

"Is that what you've been giving everybody?" asked the chairman.

The corpses began to pile up.

"No matter how obvious it is, you never use the words 'acidic' or 'iron' when people complain that their laundry or fixtures are being stained," I fired from the hip. "It's like the story about the man who called his doctor and said, 'I have a runny nose, a sore throat and a cough.' 'You may have been kicked by an ostrich,' says the doctor. 'No, there aren't any of those around,' says the man. 'Maybe your telephone wires are wrapped around your big toe,' says the doctor. 'No, we don't have a telephone,' says the man. 'Perhaps you've been stepped on by a brontosaurus,' says the doctor. 'Maybe I have a cold,' says the man. 'I never thought of that,' says the doctor.''

My opponents dodged. Through the gunsmoke the chairman agreed iron and acid content are contributing factors to the staining problems. He also agreed to tell the truth to the public in the future.

"This is a statement you're willing to have published in the paper?" I asked.

"Yes," he said with relief.

He then agreed we need a study of the water system to determine where any possible corrosive materials might be coming from and how to correct any problems that might be found. He also agreed to work with a possible committee to do something about correcting these water problems.

"Then I'll pay my water bill," I announced pompously, as I pulled out a checkbook.

I even had a pen handy, one that actually worked, although it was smoking slightly. I presented my check to the clerk.

"I'll have to put this important document in the safe," she said, chuckling.

"With my luck, it'll bounce," I said.

"Don't worry about the extra interest," she said.

A man approached me and announced in a loud voice, "I think you should demand a letter from the Water Department apologizing for the way they've treated you."

"No," I said, sounding phony. "I only want to help people."

I've accomplished what I set out to do, I said to myself as I limped away, mounted my horse and rode off—a lone silhouette against the sky. But my spies are everywhere. If the Water Department starts to stall and evade the truth, I may have to return.

At that moment I seemed to hear a voice calling after me, "Shane, Shane. Come back, Shane."

WHAT'S AN ORIGINAL PRINT

A FEW years ago, in the country's leading print magazine, I read an article entitled "What's An Original Print?" After about 20 pages of labyrinthine prose, the author of the piece came to the conclusion: "Nobody knows." Of course, there are thousands of fine printmakers in the country who create their own works with their own hands. More power to them! However, the public should know about many of the *strange* things going on in the print netherworld.

I, myself, was lured into this shadowy area a few years ago. My framer told me all about it.

"You don't have to do a thing," he said. "Chromists will copy your paintings onto plates or silkscreens. You'll get a fee of several thousand dollars per image, plus royalties. How can you lose?"

"But is it ethical?" I asked naively.

"Ethical, smethical," he said. "Who knows? Everyone is doing it. Do you think Leroy Neiman makes his own prints? His paintings are transferred to silkscreens by others. Do it. You'll make a fortune."

Greed conquered conscience, and I decided to give it a try. Strict moralists will be pleased by the outcome, which tends to sound something like *Star Wars*. I, naive Bob Skywalker, signed a contract with an agent, Bjorn Loser. He showed me around his beautiful print gallery and his spacious office. I was very impressed. Then he introduced me to E2D2, who was to execute my "original Vickreys." "Execute" has more than one meaning.

"E2 is the fastest chromist in the business," said Bjorn. "And the *best*," he added hastily. "You should see the Norman Rockwells he does. His Picassos are even better."

"Picassos?" I questioned.

"Sure, you don't think all these Picassos are done by Picasso? Of course, he's been dead for years. In some cases I know of, the prints are executed by students just out of art school. We expect to have eight Vickrey prints ready by the end of the year."

"But it's October," I said.

"Trust me," he said confidently, as he drove off in his beautiful new car.

E2 produced two prints quickly. One was fair. The other was so bad that Bjorn refused to pay the printer's bill. E2 had illegally authorized the printing of the entire edition without the permission of Bjorn or myself. Evidently he thought if he presented us with a fait accompli, we would be forced to accept his work. The printer still has all these, unless he's selling them as illegal "pirated" prints.

Meanwhile, E2 and Bjorn (yes, Bjorn himself, who has had no training as an artist) were working on the other plates together.

"Don't worry," he said. "We'll still have eight of them out by the end of the year."

"But it's December," I said.

"Look at Andy Warhol," said Bjorn. "He can turn out a whole edition in a few days. He simply takes a Polaroid photograph of the subject and has the image mechanically transferred to silkscreens which are printed onto whatever surface he chooses in his studio, which he calls "The Factory.""

"Do you seriously expect to have eight editions by the end of the year?" I asked.

"Trust me," sad Bjorn, as he strolled off in his beautifully tailored clothes.

Bjorn and I finally agreed the one print available needed more work. I agreed to try it myself.

"Good," said Bjorn. "Your royalties will be up two-and-one-half-percent. I figure you should make about two million dollars altogether."

"Tell me about the tooth fairy," I said!

After I had worked on the image for several months, I agreed to sign it. After all, I had spent more time on it than E2D2, who had left the country. It seems he was making Georgia O'Keeffe prints without her knowledge.

A different printer in New York ran off this edition of my work and held it hostage for several months until Bjorn could pay his bills.

"When do I get some royalties?" I asked.

"Trust me," he said adjusting his expensive hi-fi.

At this point, I taped two aluminum sheets to the wall of my studio and drew on them with a wax crayon. The results were better than I expected.

Remember, however, that they were single plate drawings. At any rate, my original Vickreys were *much* better than E2D2's original Vickreys. A Boston printer, H3PO, complimented me on my plates and said he would print them as soon as Bjorn paid him. This, of course, took another six months.

Soon, Bjorn was in touch with a tax shelter agency which we shall call Darth Vader Fine Arts.

"They plan to produce twenty-two Vickrey tax-shelter prints. You'll get a big fee, half in advance, half when you finish. You don't have to do a thing except sign them and pick up your check. You know, Salvador Dali signs thousands of sheets of *blank* paper. The prints are executed by somebody else at a later date. We should both make a fortune out of this."

"Umm," I said, greed and disbelief vying for supremacy in my mind. "By the way, where's your car?"

"That was a rental," he said. "I don't dare own anything."

A few weeks later, he announced I should go to Boston and start the first tax-shelter print with H3PO.

"What happened to the skilled chromist who was supposed to do it?" I asked.

"Remember, you'll get an extra two-and-a-half-percent if you do it yourself," said Bjorn quickly. "Besides Darth Vader hasn't come up with our advance, but it's due any day."

"Well, I'll give it a try," I sighed. "But I don't know what I'm doing."

"Trust me," said Bjorn.

It soon turned out Darth Vader Fine Arts was quite a notorious organization. Rumor had it their profit margin was based on the fact that they never paid their bills. They allegedly owed millions of dollars to printers, artists, and credit card companies, who had been waiting for years. Bjorn had to deal with a Darth Vader agent named Blarney San Soulo, who singlehandedly, like the Dutch boy with his finger in the dike, held back vast seas of angry artists and printers. When Bjorn tried to get our promised advances and expenses, Blarney came up with excuses like:

"It's in the mail."

"We don't have a proper address."

Secretary on the telephone: "Blarney's in Paris." (His voice could be heard in the background.)

"All checks must be signed by two Darth Vader executives at the same time. However, they're never in the office at the same time."

"We sent it to the wrong address."

"My answering service never tells me anything."

Blarney organized these few simple themes into a full symphony of deceit.

Years passed. The print I was working on was unsuccessful, since I had no knowledge in this area. Blarney came through about eight months later with the wrong amount of money sent to an inaccurate address. Eventually this print was made from scratch by somebody else.

Meanwhile, back in New York, Bjorn had found a new printer (Jabba the Hutt, Inc.) who was willing to produce the next edition.

"They are the most disreputable company in the U.S." said Bjorn. "But they will do it for nothing, as long as we use them for the future editions."

"When do I get my two million?" I asked!

"You won't get that much all at once, but Blarney says your check is in the mail."

"O.K.," I said.

The Hutt Agency (several months later) came up with a moderately acceptable silkscreen print and agreed to run off the whole edition—at almost double the amount that was in the budget. When Bjorn refused to pay, the printer washed out the screens, thus destroying several months' work.

"He has probably run off a pirated edition at a very low price, which will do your reputation no good. Maybe we can have the prints done as photographic reproductions. After all, before he died, Nelson Rockefeller had his entire collection of paintings photographed. The reproductions of these works sell for (in some cases) more than he paid for the paintings. Even Andrew Wyeth has prints on the market which are magazine-type photographic reproductions of his paintings, signed by him. He gets as much as $5000 for one of these," said Bjorn.

"Oh, well," I mused. "As long as I get my two million. I'll call you in a few days."

"Don't call me at the gallery," said Bjorn. "I'm no longer associated with it."

Next I heard from an entirely different agent and printer in Colorado. The owner of the business had a rather violent temper and reminded me of the movie character, Rocky. We'll call him Dino Mite. He agreed to produce all the remaining editions (now shrunk from 22 to 5).

"As long as we get our advance from Darth Vader," said Dino.

"Lots of luck," I said.

A year passed.

"Your work is too difficult to reproduce," said Dino. "You'll have to come to Colorado to work on the silkscreens. Blarney says that Darth Vader will pay all your expenses."

And if I clap, Tinkerbell will come back to life, I thought.

Eventually I ended up at Mite, Ltd., where I worked from 9 a.m. to (sometimes) 10 p.m., without pay, much less my $2 million. I was constantly chastised by everyone for not being cheerful.

Each day I heard hot-tempered Dino on the phone, pleading with Blarney in New York for the promised money.

He was told: "It's in the mail . . . Blarney's in Paris . . . We don't have your proper address . . ."

After two weeks, I finished and signed three editions. Blarney showed up in Colorado and promised several more things. When he left, Darth Vader had still not paid Dino, who had a gun and threatened to shoot anyone who tried to take the finished prints from him. Meanwhile, H3PO refused to answer the phone when Darth Vader called. He stalled for several months after not receiving *his* promised payment. We were all learning.

Eons later, Blarney made several more promises, some of which he kept. I mentioned all this to my lawyer, Marty Ben Kenobe.

"Don't be hard on Blarney," he said. "He's really a pussycat. He only does these things because it's part of the job."

"You are what you do," I thought with singular lack of originality.

At this point, I was approached by Tamarind Institute (this name is real) in New Mexico, the finest and most ethical print establishment in the country. They were properly horrified by these tales. But that's another story. I made three prints with them—all done the old-fashioned way—by my own hand. I felt human again.

Soon, Dino Mite went bankrupt and disappeared with one of the editions. At least he didn't *shoot* anyone.

The government then tried (more or less) to put Darth Vader out of business, claiming all their enterprises were of questionable legality. Tax-shelter owners started to sue the company.

We artists and printers now find ourselves in an unusual position: Darth Vader needs something from *us* more than we need something from *them*. I tried to contact Bjorn about this, but his office phone has been disconnected. He is currently working out of his apartment. He doesn't respond to phone calls or letters.

Blarney's secretary calls to find out where the prints are and what condition they are in. Lean and hard fighters now, we say:

"They're in the mail."

"They must have been sent to the wrong address."

"H3PO's answering service never tells him anything."

"Bob Skywalker and/or Dino Mite are in Paris."

We have been taught by masters.

ALFRED HITCHOCK ON CRYSTAL LAKE

"**D**ADDY, there's a dead naked lady stuck in the mud at the bottom of the lake," shouted a neighbor's son.

Like characters in a Hitchcock film, his whole family rushed down to the waterfront. After a few minutes of frantic diving, they found the body.

Now that I've built up the suspense, I'll backtrack a bit. Marjorie and I now live on Crystal Lake. For decades we and our four children used to come to this delightful pond. The town swimming classes traditionally thrashed about in its clear waters. Two public beaches were always thronged with happy, noisy bathers.

"Can we live on Crystal Lake some day?" our children asked.

"Perhaps," we replied.

Of course, some of the residents disapproved of the loud, cheerful sounds generated by these celebrants. An angry lady, who lived next to one public beach, complained often to the police. When she received no result, she executed her own diabolical revenge by systematically taking her large dog into the lake a few feet from the bathers and soaping it with loving, oleaginous care.

We eventually fulfilled our dream and bought a house on this lovely body of water. Our large dock had been improperly primed and was completely rotten. We replaced it with a brand new extra-long structure, which extended far out into the water.

Then the trouble began.

Attractive little ducks swam by to examine our beautiful pier. Some climbed onto it—and did what ducks do. Then the Canada Geese came, like flying Shetland ponies—doing what geese do. Next the seagulls came, doing . . . Well, at least these different types of birds were strict segregationists. They *never* mingled. The seagulls' neighborhood was on the east side of the lake. The ducks stayed in the north section. Geese preferred the west.

We heard that a kind elderly lady to the north of us was feeding our winged friends. In fact, she was buying *truckloads* of grain every week for this purpose. The geese were spending the winter in Orleans, even when the water was frozen solid. Seagulls no longer attended the botulistic smorgasbord of the town dump. My son Sean revenged himself on the polluting fowl by ice skating and crashing into their midst like a bowling ball before they could take off. You might say, he was adding a new meaning to the term "duck pins." Neighbors cautioned this humane lady about the disastrous effects of her activities. She, in turn, agreed to feed only the ducks—no geese, no seagulls.

Now we had only this *one* species to combat. Each person who owned a dock or a float constructed his own defense system. One situated a midget Indian statue (left over from a moccasin ad) to guard the premises. Another placed huge swinging arms which moved with the wind and knocked our slack-boweled friends off. A third strung clothes lines with torn flapping linen. We used pinwheels which jingled and spun with every breeze. When this didn't work, we thought of placing a loudspeaker on the dock, which would constantly broadcast the sounds of foxes, wolves and hawks. Our three-legged dog, Webster, was taught to attack whenever he heard the words, "Ducks, Webbie, ducks." He would charge ferociously to the waterfront at any hour of day or night to repulse the invaders.

Still they came.

Every time we tried a new trick, the ducks would send a spy to analyze the situation. He would swim slowly by several times, studying things. Then he would return to headquarters and (no doubt chuckling at our feeble efforts) make his report. Shortly afterward, the troops would arrive en masse.

I mentioned this warfare to the editor of the local paper. He wrote an article about the problem. Some genius came up with the headline *Vickrey's Slippery Dock*.

Residents formed a committee to combat these hordes. The duck lady, not understanding our main concern, joined the group. Nobody was brave enough to divulge to her the object of our committee. However, at the urging of friends, she agreed to feed only the ducks that came out of the water onto her lawn, which soon became a vast expanse of slime and guano.

A sort of green moss now covered the entire bottom. Town swimming classes were transferred to a nearby lake. The lady agreed to feed only the ducks she could call by name. Unfortunately, she knew multitudes.

One by one, people began taking in their docks and floats. We tried one last ruse. From an antique store I purchased a dummy, clad demurely in hoop skirt and bonnet. I nailed her to our dock in a standing position and waited. Our friend the spy-duck came by to look over the new adversary. He noticed, after several passes, that she didn't move. Soon he and his cohorts were back nuzzling the friendly petticoats.

Then vandals (human, that is) began *their* work. Every few days an article of clothing would disappear from our Victorian lady. Within weeks she was completely naked. I thought of putting one of Marjorie' bathing suits on her for decency's sake, but I figured this would also be stolen. Anyway, I went down to the dock every day and put her in a different position: in a beach chair, standing, sunning herself on her back. We got *lots* of visitors on that one. They came cautiously (like the spy-duck) to see what was going on. Finally Sean hanged her from a tree. The traffic was *overwhelming*.

More docks were withdrawn. Since every object on the lake was now covered with our winged friends, the situation became apocalyptic—like Alfred Hitchcock's *The Birds*. After all, the moral of that film is that human complacency must give way to the forces of nature.

Then, sadly, the duck lady passed on to a better world. The geese seldom stopped by now. The ducks ceased to be a concern. And the seagulls took over! Remember, they live on the rotting food from the town dump and come by our beautiful lake to bathe.

At a recent town meeting I was surprised to hear some of the speakers say, "The bird problem on Crystal Lake has been solved." All I know is that next year we are *not* putting out our dock.

Oh, yes. Our nudist dummy blew away in a hurricane one night. Two years later we heard where she was from our neighbor. She was the dead naked lady stuck in the mud.

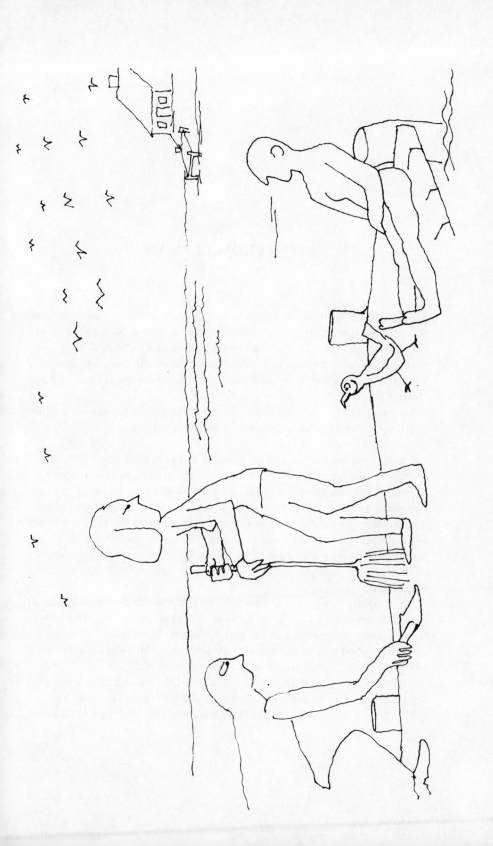

NOTES FROM ELFDOM

I REMEMBER Christmas from the old Frank Capra movies. "Every time a bell rings another angel gets his wings," chanted Jimmy Stewart's kids in *It's A Wonderful Life*. Donna Reed looked on, beaming approval. Even the town curmudgeons dropped by to contribute to the merriment. Santa himself was usually portrayed by a saintly old actor like Edmund Gwenn in *The Miracle On 34th St*.

My daughter has been an official elf for five years in the Santa's workshop of a large department store. She tells a slightly different story.

Much of the toy floor is torn up annually and converted into a vast maze of channels and railings, which resemble nothing so much as a tinsel-covered version of the Chicago stock yards. Unwary parents may be fooled by the complicated passages. One false step and they end up in the fast lane, where they speed triumphantly past the slower moving customers. They get their come-uppance, however, when they find themselves back in the doll department, after only a glimpse of the multiple Santas through the multiple windows of the multiple little cottages. Nobody tells them about this until it's too late.

My daughter is actually a moonlighting elf. She has a serious job in a respected firm for 11 months of the year. She takes leave every December for a short while to indulge in the guilty pleasures of elfdom. "I thought it might be a good way to meet men," she told me, "But unfortunately most of the elves and Santas are 19 or 20. The oldest is 30."

Santa's world is not as simple as it used to be, she tells me. Black parents began to complain because there were no black Santas. The store hastily hired a few. The elves (already happily integrated) were advised to channel

172

black customers to the black Santas. Cries of Jim Crowism arose on all sides. Then the elves were told to be strictly impartial. Luckily the kids didn't care what color their Santas were.

Other problems arose. One mother with a four-year-old child complained about the nineteen-year-old Santa to whom she was sent. "He's only a little older than my kid," she said. "The oldest Santa on duty today is twenty-two," said Elf-Carri. "You'll have to go through the line again to get to *him*." "Expletive deleted," said the lady. "Same to you," said Elf-Carri.

"I'm an atheist," said the next mother, looking the juvenile Santa in the eye. "I want you to tell my son that you're an ordinary man. There is *no* Santa Claus." "Madam, I am a method actor, and I feel that I *am* Santa," he said." I'll not betray my trust." "I want my present," said the child, as he nestled uncomfortably in the tiny lap. "You've already paid for it," said Elf-Carri, helpfully, as she hurried them on their way. "Next," she called, massaging her bunions, since elves never get to sit down.

"Hey, we want our picture," said an irate mother. "$6.00 a print," said the Elf-Photographer, stepping from the papier-mâché fireplace. "Next door they only charge $5.00," said the mother. "But *here* we accept Mastercard and Visa," said the Elf-Photographer. "You should bring your own camera," whispered Elf-Carri. "Are you planning to be here next year?" hissed the Elf-Photographer. "Not if *you're* here," countered Elf-Carri. "Some people order as many as one hundred prints of my pictures," said the Elf-Photographer, huffily.

"What's holding up the line," called an angry father through the tiny window which was two feet off the ground. "Try another cottage," said Santa, whose voice had just changed. "They're all jammed up, too," shouted the father, pushing his fist through the acetate window. "Watch it," called Santa. "I've got 27 elves here, some of them professional wrestlers."

"He's known as the Captain Queeg of Santas," whispered Elf-Carri to the mother, "And I think he's got this place bugged." "I want my present," cried the child. "Please stop tearing the acetate," said Elf-Carri, adjusting her pointed ears.

A different Santa and several different elves came on duty. "Remember," one of them said to my daughter who was departing. "No smoking or eating in costume." "We tiny folks try to obey all the rules," said a six-foot elf, ducking his head to enter the cottage.

Elves, it seems, are the underdogs of the Christmas world. Santas have their own dressing room with lockers for their beards and paunches. They even have hairdressers. Elves must put on their costume and apply their make-up in the employees' bathroom. They also have to supply their own shoes. Daily notices are posted if they're caught eating or smoking in costume.

Santas are fully insured for arthritic backs, flaming beards, water on the knee, etc. Elves are not so lucky. One elf, whose nose was broken in the crush of celebrants, applied for medical coverage. "We have no insurance for damaged elves," said the management.

One of the Santas was quite evangelical. "Your parents are always right," he often said. "*Always* do what they tell you." "I want my present," said the kid. "Santa is always watching you," he continued. "Just like Big Brother," sighed Carri to herself.

Some of the atheist parents complained about the Christmas carols being played over the loudspeaker, so the store changed its policy and repeated the *Nutcracker Suite* continuously.

"Tell your kid to stop feeling my paunch to see if it's real. Also tell him to stop pulling my beard down," said the Santa. "Maybe if you were old enough to shave," said the parent. "I do—every other day," replied the Santa.

"Next," called Carri, returning from the criminal practice of eating a candy bar in costume. "I smell Milky Way on your breath," said Queeg Santa, who was back on duty. "KGB," mumbled Elf-Carri, plopping a plump child onto the skinny lap and slipping a paper with the child's name into Santa's gloved hand. "What do you want for Christmas, Jimmy?" asked Santa. "How did you know my name?" countered the child. "We Santas know everything," said Queeg Santa, rattling three little metal balls in his left hand.

Later, a hippy Santa came on duty. A sad child arrived holding the hand of her lonely looking father. "I want an atomic bomb," she announced. "Now," said Santa, trying to read Carri's handwriting, "Uuuh, Edna, why do you want that?" "Daddy says we all need one," she said angelically. Santa paused, adjusted his hat (showing his long blond locks), and began a plea for peace. "God is love," he said.

"Hey, it's ten thirty at night," called someone through the torn window. "First things come first," said Santa, patiently beginning the story of mankind. "There are others waiting," said a beautiful female elf, who had just come on duty. "I have to have her back to her mother by eleven," said the obviously divorced father.

"The store is going to close soon," came the shout through the window. "O.K., O.K.," said the divorced father as he and his child hurried out of the styrofoam cottage, almost knocking over the Elf-Photographer in the fireplace. "Here's my card," said the beautiful elf, adjusting her blouse. "I'm available at all hours, except when I'm here, of course."

"I'm getting awfully sick of the 'Nutcracker Suite'," said Carri.

The next Santa refused to remove his sunglasses. "That's my image," he kept saying as he snapped his fingers. "I want a Cabbage Patch doll," said the little girl in his lap. "What the heck is that, Baby Jane?" he sang out.

"In his condition, he wouldn't know a Smurf from a Cookie Monster," said the beautiful elf, handing another of her cards to a lone father. "There's a lady Santa in cottage three," said the beautiful elf. She knows all about Smurfs and Cabbage Patchers." "I'll give it a try," said the father, hastily shoving the card into a pocket.

"I don't want a lady Santa," said the child. "Does she have a beard?" asked the father, waiting to see if Carri would hand him a card. "Yes," said Carri, glancing at the styrofoam cuckoo clock which read eleven o'-clock. "For awhile we had a Mrs. Santa in an apron and a bonnet, but the Women Libbers objected. So now we have a lady Santa with a beard and all. There's no sexism here." "Thanks," said the departing father. "You all come back now," called the beautiful elf after him.

"I'm not sure I'm going to do this next year," said Carri.

FILE ON MATA CARRI

My daughter tells me that it's hard meeting men in New York, so she decided to place an ad in the "Personals" column of a famous magazine:

Pretty, Witty and Wise—vivacious
female, with marvelous hug, seeks
bright, humorous man to share
   movies,
the arts, adventure. Photo please.
Box 007.

She brought it into the office the next day and convinced two colleagues to invest in this venture with her. They wondered which one would be Pretty, which Witty and which Wise.

"We'll work that out later," they agreed.

Carri called the magazine and placed the ad. A stern voice insisted on correct punctuation, which meant inserting several commas—and increasing the cost by another $20.

Carri expressed some concern over the fact that all this strange mail would be sent to *her* office. She was assured that it would arrive in plain, brown envelopes.

Two weeks passed. Letters started pouring in. Most correspondents claimed to be at least six feet tall. One man gave his height in inches.

Many said "This is the first time I've ever done this."

Their letters, however, were usually xeroxed. An ophthalmologist's writing was so small, she needed a magnifying glass to read it. A holistic physician recorded his weight as "depending on my last meal". Under the heading "Religion" he wrote: "Pritikin Program."

With the letters came pictures. A dentist sent a copy of his molar x-rays. A policeman sent a photograph that had obviously been cut in half. The three girls noticed a few blond curls still resting on his shoulder from the female who had been deleted. The stock broker sent a *nude* photograph of himself posing in front of his motorboat. He asked that the photograph be returned. They sent him back a photostat. The jazz musician enclosed a program from his last performance. The chiropractor wanted Carri to send him a picture of her with her parents. He wanted to know if their backs were straight.

There was a letter that began "Would you move to Alaska?" Included was a note from the man's mother. "All he needs is a nice wife," she said. "I know you'll like my son." It was signed "CM".

"What does that mean?" asked Pretty.

"Concerned Mother, I guess," said Witty.

The dentist knew hundreds of jokes. "May the floss be with you," was his best.

"I wonder what his worst is like," said Witty.

"He's anxious to hear *our* baby's first words," said Pretty.

"Next letter, please," said Wise.

"This one is addressed To Agent 007, not Box 007," said Pretty.

"It looks like a script," said Witty. "It *is*. It's written in the format of *Mission Impossible*."

The joker in the photograph described himself as a "Notorious Russian Spy Attempting to Irradicate Sugar Substitutes and Change the Course of American History." The margins of the next letter were filled with humorous asides like, "Ouch, what a hug!, "Oh, you animal!, and "Oooh, that smarts!" An account executive listed all his relationships for the last ten years. "Man looking for non-control-oriented woman" wanted to hear from Carri only if she fulfilled *his* requirements. He was looking for a "traditional relationship and a glorious up-scale existence on Park Avenue."

With so much sterling material to choose from, they began to argue.

"I want the holistic physician," said Pretty.

"Oh, no you don't," said Witty. "He's mine. You take the Alaskan with the Concerned Mother."

"Fat chance," said Wise. "I get goose bumps in August."

"How about the dentist with the great sense of humor?" said Pretty.

"Hey. What's that you locked in that drawer?" said Witty.

"Just a note from my mother," said Pretty.

"Since when does she use a plain brown envelope?" said Witty. "Also, some of these letters seem to have been opened already."

It was beginning to seem like a James Bond movie.

"We agreed to open them together," said Pretty.

"And no fair xeroxing," said Witty, trying to slip one into her pocket.

"You always get to the office first in the morning," snapped Wise. "How do we know you don't steal some of the best ones?"

"I'll trade you three lawyers for the nice-looking policeman," said Pretty.

"No, we *all* want him," came the chorus.

"What about those blond hairs on his shoulder?" asked Pretty.

"Maybe they were his mother's," said Witty.

"After all, it *was* a black and white photograph," said Wise.

"Why don't you take the naked boatsman?" said Pretty. "At least we know he doesn't dye his hair."

"No," came the unanimous chorus.

"There were 27 letters here a few minutes ago," said Pretty. "Now I count 18."

"Do you suggest a strip search?" asked Witty.

"We've got to trust each other," said Wise.

Several men asked to be called at home *after* 10 p.m.

"I guess they're workaholics," said Pretty.

"Or they're afraid of what their secretaries will think," said Witty.

"Or their mothers," said Wise.

Word of what they were doing leaked out. Everyone came to give advice.

"You should check the addresses and numbers in the phone book," suggested one.

"Try calling them during the day to see if there's a wife," said another.

"If they have an answering machine at least you can hear what they sound like," said a third.

Most of their dates took them to inexpensive Chinese restaurants. Pretty's first date was "Writer-Painter-Deal-Maker". His photograph had shown him standing in front of a large painting of a zebra. Wise dated a "Tall Preppie Caterer". His letter had been peppered with humorous status symbols: Ivy League education, house in the Hamptons, and a golden retriever named Kiki.

"I'd like to have a reference," said Witty. "Could you bring the dog along?" On the day of their date, he called to cancel. Kiki was sick.

Wise phoned "Handsome, Six-Foot, Stockbroker".

"Exactly what does a stockbroker do?" she asked.

"Let's talk about *you*," he said quickly.

"I'm working nights as an elf at Macy's," she said.

"Just how tall are you?" he asked angrily.

"I'm not a dwarf," snapped Wise, hanging up.

Witty called "Handsome, Six-Foot Self-employed Importer of Christmas Ornaments". They met at the Ee Khan O Mee restaurant. The waiter approached.

"Hello, Joe," said her five foot date.

"Always glad to see a regular customer," said Joe, eyeing Witty suspiciously.

After several martinis, her date excused himself, got up and passed out. .

"No mono-sodium-glutamate tonight," sighed Witty.

Next, she dated "Good-looking Six-Foot Ex-contestant from *The Price Is Right*."

"What exactly do you do?" she asked, looking down at his bald spot.

"Oh, I write a little, I paint a little . . . You know," he said, rocking back on his elevator shoes.

"In other words, you're unemployed," said Witty.

"Do you like Chinese food?" he asked quickly.

"I guess so," said Witty.

At Ee Khan O Mee, Joe approached and took their order.

Later, Wise noticed that for the first time in her life, Pretty was arriving at the office earlier and earlier.

"She's never been on time before in her life," Wise remarked.

"Do you suppose—?" mused Witty.

"Maybe the early bird is catching the worms." said Wise.

"No comment," said Witty.

On the following day Witty came in *very* early and hid behind a cabinet. Sure enough, Pretty sneaked in and started feeling the mail. Since it was common knowledge that only the best looking men sent photographs, it was easy to *feel* which letters were from the most desirable ones. Pretty hid these choice items in her desk and went triumphantly out. Witty removed the letters, took them to the coffee maker, and steamed them open. She then xeroxed them and carefully replaced them.

Wise noticed that the quality of *her* respondents was sinking rapidly, so she bribed the mail clerk to let her go through the mail when it first arrived in the mail room at 7 a.m.

"I'll try once more," said Witty, gloomily.

She and her date settled into their booth at Ee Khan O Mee. Joe eyed her angrily. Her date, "Attractive, Six-Foot, Window Dresser" examined his hands and complained about the filth on the subways.

"Excuse me. I have to go wash," he said as he left.

Joe edged closer.

"Don't bring any more of your clients here," he hissed.

Witty hurried out of the restaurant without washing *her* hands.

Eventually, Pretty, Witty, and Wise received an invitation to a party from "Handsome, Six-Foot *Chorus Line* Extra".

"You'll see a lot of friends," he said.

Our threesome were greeted at the door by a number of Pee Wee Herman look-a-likes. Their host, a small bug-eyed man, took Pretty's hand.

Nibbling delicately, he whispered in her ear, "You're the most beautiful woman at this party."

They moved to the snack table surrounded by six Clairol #2 blondes.

"I guess this is our competition," sighed Witty, as the bug-eyed man whispered into her ear, "You're the most beautiful woman at this party."

Several gentlemen introduced themselves to each other and exchanged cards.

"What next," groaned Witty.

Wise tried to disengage herself from the short, bug-eyed man who was making the final assault upon *her* ear. He had to stand on tip toes.

She started, looking at him closely, and gasped, "My God. You're 'Sexy, Nude, Six-Foot Boater'! I didn't recognize you with your clothes on."

At this remark the whole room turned and faced them.

"There's Zebra Man'," gasped Pretty.

"And that's 'Hugable Preppie Caterer'," moaned Witty. *"And* his dog, Kiki."

"There's 'Holistic Para-pyschologist'," said Wise.

"Why, they're all *rejects*," cried Pretty.

"Well," said Witty, "What does that make us?"

A YUPPY CHRISTMAS

Who says that Americans are culturally deprived? We probably hear more great music every day than any people in the world. Scenes like the following are taking place all over the United States.

In the suburbs Jack Smith is returning from the office.

"Hi Honey, I'm home. What's for dinner?" he calls out.

"Vienna Schnitzle?" answers his wife Jill.

"Ah, so that's why you're listening to Mozart," he says.

"Am I?" she replies.

"Sure. I heard *Eine Kleine Nachtmusik* as I came in. A little touch of Tom Hulce in the night."

"That was the *Dr. Pepper* commercial. They have it for background music."

"Well, that's what it was originally written for."

"Okay, Okay, Mr. Male-Chauvinist-Know-It-All. Anyway, I got the recipe from *Cook's* magazine."

"Just because you like show music doesn't mean you shouldn't enjoy Mozart . . . or Vivaldi. *Cook's* magazine is using *The Four Seasons*."

"Dinner will be a little late," she says grumpily. "I don't like the classics. I'm going to listen to *my* records."

"I'll take a nap," he mutters.

Half an hour later Jill calls out, "Dinner's ready.

"I enjoyed some of your selections," he says, waking up, "Especially *Food, Glorious Food* from *Oliver*."

"No, that was *Cheese, Glorious Cheese*."

"*Hello Dolly* was good too."

182

"That was the *Hello Deli* commercial for *Oscar Meyer* weiners. Actually, my record player seems to be broken."

"Didn't I hear Sondheim's *Something Familiar?*"

"That was *Stove Top* stuffing." she says, losing patience.

"And I thought I heard *Baby Face*. Don't tell me they can make anything out of *that*."

" *'Baby Pants*, you've got the sweetest little *Baby Pants.'* It's a disposable deodorant diaper jingle."

"Is nothing sacred?"

"Here's your dinner," she says. "You like *your* music, I like *mine*."

"Now I'm getting indigestion."

"Try some Brioschi."

"No. Then I'll just keep hearing their TV theme, *Sur le Pont D'Avignon*," he starts to sing, "Eat too much, drink too much. Try Brioschi! Try Brioschi!"

"I think we need a new car."

"Which composers do you like?"

"What does that remark mean?"

"Well, if you want a Baroque feel to your driving, you could get a Porsche. They have one of Bach's *Brandenburg Concertos* as background music. See, there it is *now*."

"That's the *Grey Poupon* mustard commercial."

"If *those* go on long enough, we'll get to hear the complete Brandenburgs."

"Maybe we should get a Honda Civic."

"Honey, you're a true romantic," he says, kissing her, *"They're* using Tchaikovsky's *Romeo and Juliet* overture. By the way, did you feed the cat?"

"What brought that up?"

"I just heard the Friskies ad—with Beethovan's *Sixth Symphony*. Do cats like Beethovan?"

"I thought that was the *Cordon Nin* champagne theme."

"It *is*. They're *both* stealing from Ludwig Van. Hey, let's break out the champagne while we're at it. We need a little Christmas cheer. Oops, don't spill it."

"Keep your hands to yourself," she giggles, "And give me some more."

"Don't finish it off! Tomorrow is Christmas. The liquor store will be closed."

"We still have some *Sun Country Cooler*. I got it because I like the background music. You know the piece. The one the organists in the movies play when they go insane."

"Bach's *Toccata and Fugue in D-Minor*. Disney used it in *Fantasia*. You know, now *Burger King* is using it. Uh, oh, the champagne is all gone."

"We have another bottle under the tree," she says shakily, "How about some dessert? We have *Frusan Gladge*."

"Yes, yes," he says groggily, "I love that Bocherini string quartet. *Enjoy the guilt*", he chortles, "That wife is *so* weak-willed. Not like *you*, of course."

He starts to sing, "*La Donna e Mobile*."

"I know that," she says, jumping onto the table, "It's the *Franchesca Rinaldi* jingle."

"*O Chi Chiornia*," he sings, jumping up beside her.

"That's the *Real Cheese* commercial. And there's my favorite of all time. The wonderful *Cue-tips* jingle," she calls as the table collapses.

"I know, I know . . . Rossini's *Overture to the Thieving Magpie*."

"Anyway, Merry Christmas, darling," she says sinking down beside him. "Hey, don't pass out. They're finally playing Christmas carols."

"Yeah. I love *Joy To The World*."

"No, no, that's *Soy To The World* . . ."

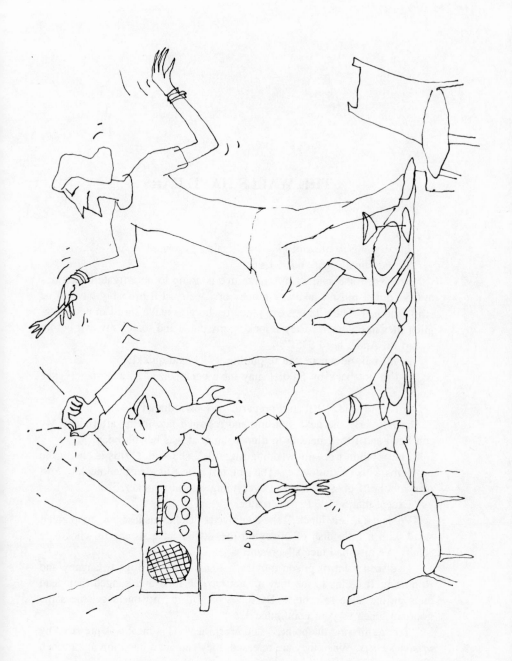

THE WALLS HAVE EARS

"I'M going to prison tomorrow," said Marjorie.

"So they finally got you," I said.

"No. No." she said. "My committee is going to investigate conditions at Concord. I musn't take any money or jewelry. I'll probably have to be strip-searched. They'll even examine my shoes to make sure I'm not smuggling files in my heels. They'll lock up my purse and search my hair before we go in. And I need $35."

"Don't tell me where you're putting it," I said quickly.

"If I'm not back by 5:00, I may have been seized as a hostage," she said.

"O.K.," I said. "I'll start preparing my own dinner."

She left early the next morning and returned late in the afternoon. My son Sean and I took her out to dinner, since it was her birthday.

"They couldn't get my wedding ring off," she said. "This is one of the problems with visiting wives. The ring just won't fit over the knuckle. Sort of symbolic, I guess. They put everything else in a locker."

"Except that $35," I corrected her.

"We had a lovely lunch," she continued. "Delicious lasagna, crisp green salad with a little dish of olives on the side. And a wonderful chocolate éclair. We also had nice silverware."

"I've seen a lot of prison movies," I said. "With Bogart, Cagney and Robinson. It seems to me they all got terrible food and banged their lead cups on the table to protest. By the way, did the prisoners get the same gourmet lunch as your committee?"

"You're missing the point," said Marjorie. "This meal was prepared by *prisoner chefs*. When they are released, they can get a good job in a French restaurant. *Of course* the other prisoners didn't get the same food we did.''

"Or eat with the same silverware," added Sean, ironically. "You know that's a minimum security prison. But with recidivism, these men will be back within a few months." he added.

"Then they can cook real French meals for the other inmates," I said glumly.

"No," said Sean. "Prisoners don't want French cooking."

I noticed that the family at the next table were listening to us.

"I wonder," I asked. "Do they still wear those striped suits and caps with the visors?"

"Actually," said Marjorie, "The ones I saw were all wearing jogging suits."

"That way," I mused, "when they escape, they can blend in with the other joggers in Concord. No one would be suspicious of runners dressed like that."

"No," said Marjorie. "They have 'Concord Prison' on their T-shirts."

"You mean in big, bold letters like in a Charlie Chaplin movie?" I asked.

"No, a small tasteful emblem over the heart." said Marjorie.

"I guess that gives the guards a convenient target," I said philosophically.

"Isn't it kind of cold for jogging suits?" asked Sean.

"They only wear them indoors," said Marjorie.

"You know, Walpole has solved *one* of its problems," said Sean. "The *town*, I mean. They got so sick of having people confuse the town with the prison that they changed the name of the prison. Now it's called *Cedar Junction*."

"That's like the gag about cancer and smoking," I said. "Where the man read so many articles about cigarettes causing cancer that he gave up reading. Also, what respectable professional criminal would admit that he had been sent to a place with a corny name like Cedar Junction? Alcatraz, Folsom, and Levenworth. Now *those* sound like good, tough places that any crook would be proud to acknowledge."

"You still don't understand," said Marjorie. "They're all wearing the *same* jogging suits."

"But if only one or two escape," I asked, "who would notice?"

"Well, maybe they could escape in groups," said Marjorie.

"The recidivism rate is against them." said Sean, glancing at the next table. "Very few ever escape. Most of these people are doomed."

"No," said Marjorie. "We inspected their cells. They told us that 60% are doomed. The others may survive."

"But some of them have been criminals since the age of eight." said Sean. "They don't even know any other life."

"I think every human being is salvageable," said Marjorie.

"Especially if they learn French cooking," I sighed.

Our neighbors had stopped talking completely. Their ears seemed to have grown measurably larger.

"One of the members of our group had actually been attacked twice, possibly by somebody in the prison we were seeing that day. She was very sweet, though, and forgave everyone." said Marjorie.

"You mean she may have been attacked by one of the prisoners you were interviewing?" I asked.

"Well, we never got within twenty feet of them," said Marjorie. "The prison officials didn't want us to find out *anything*. We all know, though, how bad conditions are. And they're getting worse."

"I know," I said. "If I make jokes, it's only to keep from crying. I'm afraid that well-meaning committees of this sort are not going to be allowed to do much good."

The people at the table next to us had finished their meal and paid their bill, but they made no move to leave.

"Some of the cells were so small that you could reach out and touch all the walls," said Marjorie.

"Well, at least each person had privacy," said Sean.

"No," said Marjorie. "Two, three, or even four men were in each room. Reaganomics, you know. And some of the guards of the criminally insane are now criminally insane themselves."

"You mean they're mixed together?" I asked.

"Ronald Reagan says we must take care of our own insane," said Marjorie.

"Or they must take care of us," I added.

"But the curtains on the windows were very clean," said Marjorie.

"They saw you coming," said Sean.

We left at this point, glancing back at the table whose occupants seemed to have turned to stone.

"Anyway, Happy Birthday, Mom," said Sean.

"When do I get my $35 back?" I asked.

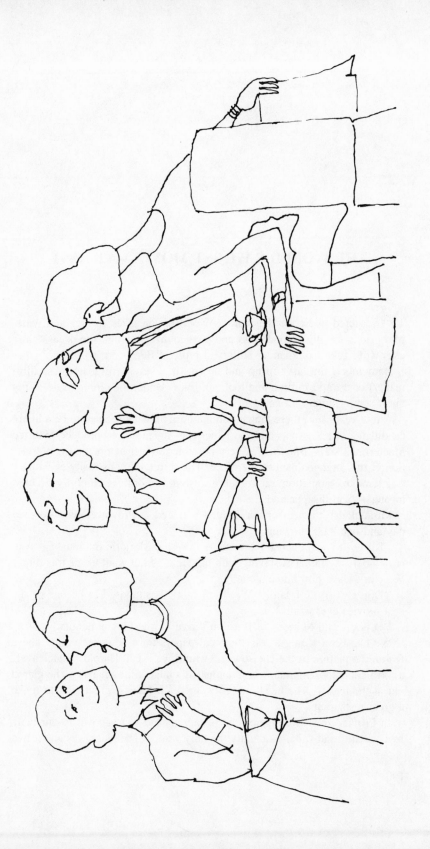

THE WORLD'S WORST MOVIE—AT LAST

M<small>Y</small> sacred quest for the world's worst movie takes me far and wide. Marjorie is usually a good sport and goes along, although she occasionally asks why. Like Commander Hillary, I reply, "Because it's *there*."

Remember, the last trip up and down Mt. Everest (by a Japanese film-maker) cost $2 ½ million and took six lives. Under the circumstances, my quest seems quite reasonable.

A few years ago, there loomed on the horizon what seemed to be a likely candidate. The Russians and the Americans agreed to co-produce Maurice Maeterlinck's *The Blue Bird*. Every possible blunder hampered the production of this strange dated theaterpiece. The resultant monstrosity eventually staggered to completion, ran for a few days in two or three carefully selected theaters—and disappeared.

Miraculously, a year or two later it surfaced in Provincetown—for one day and one 8:00 showing.

"I'll go if I can choose the restaurant," said Marjorie dubiously. "And remember, my father is staying with us. He may not want to see this thing. We can't leave him home alone."

"Don't worry," I said. "We'll tell him it's supposed to be one of the best movies ever made."

"O.K.," said Marjorie, "But don't give him too many details."

We had been seeing ads in the local papers for a new restaurant. These featured a picture of the chef-owner, whom we'll call Harold Meatcleaver, a formidable looking man who brandished a huge knife-cleaver as he glared out at the reader. The headline proclaimed "It takes a great chef to make a great restaurant."

In Provincetown we entered the restaurant and were shown to our table by a tactful headwaiter—actually the only waiter. The place was about two thirds full. We noticed that there was no door to the kitchen. "Good ambiance," I said, "The lines of communication between the feeders and the eaters will not be interrupted."

"Meatcleaver is a famous food critic," said Marjorie.

"I wonder if they make a decent martini?" said her father.

"We have several specials tonight," said the headwaiter, raising his voice slightly to cover some mild altercation in the kitchen. New customers entered and hearing the rising decibels, left in haste. Four-letter words began to color the atmosphere. Screams and shouts assailed our ears. More customers left. The headwaiter tried to mollify the remaining stalwarts.

"Harold's not himself tonight. But the *food* will still be good," he shouted. Harold rushed by the open doorway swinging a huge cleaver, no doubt the same one he displayed in the ad. The kitchen was narrow with a long table down the middle. The fleeing staff fell back before his onslaught, ducking beneath the table and trying to keep as much space as possible between themselves and the murderous arching weapon. From time to time Harold stopped and glowered through the opening and shook his weapon menacingly at the departing diners. Soon we were alone.

"I'll have another martini," said Marjorie's father firmly.

"Don't you think we'd better go?" said Marjorie.

"Let 'im come," said her father, clenching his fists, "I know how to handle this guy. I have to walk through Newark almost every day."

"Please bear with us," said the headwaiter, as a loud crash from the kitchen drowned him out. Several more helpers ducked under the long table, but we noticed that they didn't leave the kitchen.

"I guess this happens quite often," I said.

"But he's the food editor of the local paper," said Marjorie.

"Where's my martini?" called Marjorie's father.

"And he writes so beautifully," said Marjorie.

"By the way, what's this movie we're going to?" asked her father.

"Don't worry. It's a masterpiece," Marjorie and I said in unison.

Harold finally stormed out of the restaurant and stood communing with nature under our window. "At least he doesn't have his cleaver with him," said Marjorie.

Our dinner arrived—and it was *great*. Even the martini was acceptable. Later we hurried to the theatre. "I hope this is as good as you guys say," said Marjorie's father.

"We guarantee it, don't we?" I said to Marjorie.

"Mmm," she said.

There were about thirty of us aficionados present, all there for the same

reason. Remember, this was *one* show for *one* night only. The event was
—well, vestal. The audience began to howl.

We watched the antics of characters such as "Dog", "Cat", "Milk",
"Fire", and "Lust", all searching for (you guessed it) the Bluebird of
Happiness, which, of course, turns out to be in their own backyard. The
best scene takes place in the Land of the Unborn Children, where brother
and sister Tyltyl and Mytyl meet Father Time (Robert Morley), doing a
song and dance number. Next, they come upon an unborn child—who is
older than they are.

"I'm going to be your little brother," he announces.

"Oh, Mommy will be so surprised," says Mytyl.

"Don't get too excited though," says the oversized baby brother, "I'm
going to die shortly after I'm born."

"It *hardly* seems worthwhile," says Tyltyl.

"We all bring presents down to earth when we come," says another
unborn child.

"What are you bringing?" asks Mytyl, naively.

"Scarlet fever, whooping cough, and measles," he answers brightly.

The audience clapped and applauded almost constantly.

"Why are we seeing this?" asked Marjorie's father.

"Sh." we said.

The climax came. A thousand pigeons (all dyed blue) flew into the fir-
mament.

"I guess they couldn't find any real bluebirds," said Marjorie.

"*They* wouldn't be big enough," I said.

We left in a state of euphoria. "What a great experience," I said.

"You mean," said Marjorie's father, "you intellectuals really *fell* for
that stuff?"

"Look at all these happy people," I said. "They're all enjoying the
subtle, aesthetic symbolism and the intense emotional content of the imagery.
Didn't you appreciate the anthropomorphic metaphors and iconoclastic images?"

"Where can you get a martini at this time of night?" he asked.

We drove happily home, safe in the knowledge that we had at last seen
the world's worst movie.

A year or two later Marjorie and I returned to the restaurant. All was
peaceful and calm. Harold was not in evidence—and the food was *very*
dull.

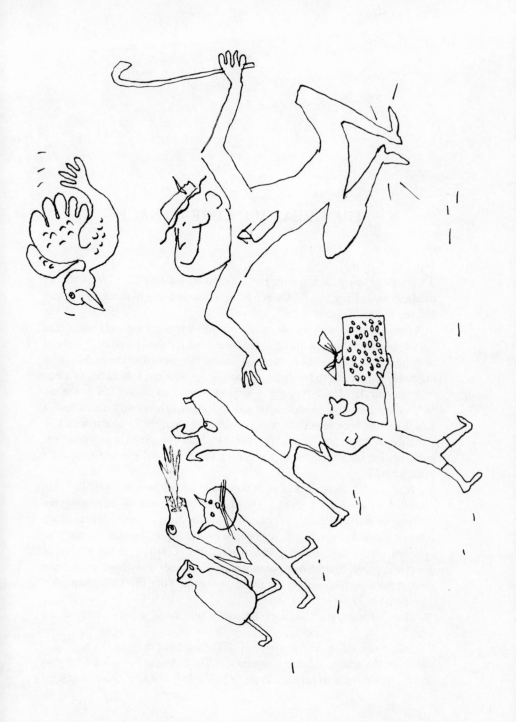

THE GREAT ICE CUBE MENACE

Recently my daughter sent me a magazine called *THE UNUSUAL*. A headline caught my eye, "Are we being ruled and manipulated by sinister and unexpected forces?"

A reproduction showed a seemingly harmless glass of gin and tonic. "Let your eyes concentrate on the third ice cube from the top," it read. "Without stretching your imagination, can you see an 'S' formed in the highlight of the cube? Down and to the right, following the texture of the lime, you can make out an 'E'. Hold the page at arm's length. You cannot fail to see the 'X', created by the condensation on the glass. Three wolf faces and a scorpion have been retouched into the cubes on the right for an extra kick."

"Hmm," I thought, "dirty ice cubes. I've been hearing about subliminal manipulation for years, but this is getting serious. If my gin and tonic isn't safe, what is?"

I read on. "You can't pick up a newspaper or a magazine without being assaulted by such an embeds. The use of this device is increasing the tendency of our civilization to commit Freudian slips, as secret desires creep into our conversations. We have become a nation of unknowing robots. Our opinions are formed, shaped, and manipulated according to the wishes of the powers that control our publications. Such messages have even been discovered superimposed on the Great Seal behind our President during his TV speeches."

"Hey," I thought, "Some of Reagan's talks *have* seemed pretty weird lately."

A magazine cover was reproduced. "The curve of the model's top lip," continued the article, "forms a capital 'S'. The crease in her lower lip forms an 'E'. The dimple in her chin is an 'X'. The locks of hair on her forehead have been touched up to spell out one of the most unmentionable of uck-words.''

"I wonder what the other one is," I thought.

A brandy ad was depicted. "If a mirror is held above the retouched shadows, the mirror image will read 'U BUY'.''

"Life will never by the same," I mused and began to imagine how it might be. . . .

"We've been invited to a party tonight," said Marjorie.

"Let me see the invitation," I said.

"It's just a normal little invitation,''

"Let me see it anyway,''

"Have you been reading that magazine again?" said Marjorie.

"Keep the corners of your mouth straight," I answered. "I can see little "S"'s and "X"'s under your lower lip.''

I looked at the invitation.

"Hi Folks, We're having a few people over for drinks at 6:00 on Friday. See ya. Regrets only.''

"You can't find anything suspicious in that," said Marjorie triumphantly.

"Wait a minute. That six looks like—you know. And those two zeros look like. . . . It's an invitation to an orgy.''

"But these are old, old friends.''

"I know what I know.''

"Oh, go paint," she said.

I took a cold shower and went to my studio where I was working on a landscape, manipulating "BUY ME. BUY ME' into the foliage. The phone rang. "Time to get ready," said Marjorie.

I couldn't see the corners of her mouth.

At the party we greeted our old, old friends, holding our mouths tight and straight. We couldn't do much about our dimples. Our hostess's ringlets were spelling out four-letter words. Our host saw this, and his mustache formed the word "Not with my wife.''

"Did you see that wonderful old movie *Irma La Douche* last night?" asked someone.

"No, we were watching Shakespeare's 'Titus Androgynous'," another replied.

"Freudian slips, Freudian slips," I said to myself.

"Could you fix me a drink?" asked a woman standing nearby.

"Sure," I said, not looking at *her* dimple.

"Scotch on the rocks," she said. I complied. "Thanks," she said. Then she looked hard and long at her ice cubes.

"You cad!" she said, flinging it in my face. Strands of hair fell across her forehead, spelling out unspeakable suggestions. As she walked away though, the folds in her skirt indicated, "Your place or mine." I quickly ordered a drink *without* ice cubes, and wandered about, keeping my eyes on the floor. "Hi, Big Boy," caught my attention from the fringes on the bottom of a dress. Sheepishly, I looked up. It was the wife of my oldest friend. She was studying my sideburns.

"Can't you think of anything else?" she snapped. Locks of her hair warned, "My husband is right behind you."

I tried making conversation for a while but everything came out sounding wrong. Some one passed the peanuts, but as I was reaching for one, I realized that they looked like . . . I pulled back my hand. The shadows in the curtains spelled out more obscenities.

"It's time to go," said Marjorie later.

We said goodbye to our hostess. Disconcerting little "S"'s and "X"'s played about her lips. Our host's mustache bristled menacingly. The ice cubes in his drink glowered at me with a lupine intensity. I noticed green-eyed monsters forming in the condensation on his glass.

Marjorie pulled me toward the door, whispering, "One more drink and you'll be prostate on the floor."

I gave her an intense look. The curls on her forehead spelled out, "Not tonight. I have a headache."

TALKING MACHINERY

A FRIEND of mine bought a camera recently. Since she knew nothing about photography, she asked for one that would do everything automatically. At home she took it from its box.

"Load film," called a squeaky voice.

"Hello, dear," she said, thinking it was her husband. "I didn't know you were home. Also, you sound as if you have a cold."

"Advance film," called the nasty little voice, almost causing her to drop the thing. "Check focus," it squealed.

"Oh, shut up," she retorted.

"It was quite insulting," she told us later.

"You know," said Tom, "they have talking cars now. They tell you when there's something wrong."

"And an ignition," said Dick, "that's sensitive to alcohol on the driver's breath."

"I know someone with a talking watch," said Harry. "It reminds you of your appointments."

"How about those talking scales in the English subways?" I asked.

"What's next?" sighed my friend.

I imagined what life in the future might be like . . .

Marjorie and I were attending the opening party at an art gallery. It was hot and most of the guests stood outside talking.

"This is getting dull," I said, "Let's go."

"O.K., I'll meet you at the car."

Knowing I had some time to kill, I decided to weigh myself on the nearby public scale. I slipped the proper coin into the slot. "178," barked the scale derisively. "Better lay off the lasagna, Fatso."

I found our car and got in. "Ugh." said the ignition, sniffing my breath.

"Remember your restaurant reservation in eighteen minutes," said my wristwatch. "By the way, you're over your credit limit," said a small voice from inside my jacket. It was my credit-card-size calculator.

"Shut up," I mumbled just as Marjorie got into the car.

"Don't be so disagreeable."

"I wasn't talking to you," I said.

"How many drinks have you had?" she asked.

"His blood alcohol level is above the acceptable limit," said my pocket calculator.

"His pulse is uneven," said my wristwatch.

"And his heartbeat is irregular," said my calculator.

I tried to slip my key into the ignition. "No way am I gonna start for someone with a breath like that," said the ignition.

"I only had two and a half—well, three drinks," I said.

"I counted seven," said the headlights.

"Also, the dunderhead forgot to get gas," said the fuel gauge.

"Please buckle up," said a metallic voice from hip level.

"Thank you for being courteous," I said.

"Your reservation is in seven minutes," said my wristwatch.

"How about if I let Marjorie drive?" I asked in desperation.

"I am monitored to refuse ignition if the air/oxygen limit of the car is above the legal limit," said the ignition.

"Don't be so pompous," said my calculator.

"Listen," I said, reaching for my pocket knife, "I know how to splice the wires and bypass you."

"Just try, and I'll smother you with my air bag," said the ignition.

"It'll take a pretty big bag for that blimpo," called out the scale.

"You keep out of this," I snapped.

"I'll signal the restaurant to cancel your reservation," said my wristwatch.

"But I'm hungry," said my wife.

"I have an idea," said my calculator. "Let the wristwatch drive."

"*That* I'll go for," said the ignition. "You two get in the back seat and maybe I'll reconsider."

"Start'er up, Buster," said my wristwatch to the ignition. "Where are the lights in this pile of junk?"

"Watch your mouth, Tinkertoy," said the ignition. "You big brains always think you're better than us proletariats."

"Don't forget to get gas," said the gauge.

My camera spoke up from beside me, "I'll keep a lookout for cops."

"I think you guys should get better organized," said my calculator as we drove off.

"Tomorrow start Weight Watchers," called out the scale. "And Alcoholics Anonymous," mumbled the ignition.

COFFEE WITH THE CANDIDATE

"**I** HOPE you're coming to meet our candidate, Mr. Dee next Tuesday morning," said Marjorie.

"I'd love to," I said quickly, "But I, uh, think my car is being repaired that day."

"It's at *our* house." said Marjorie firmly.

"I think I'm playing tennis," I said.

"Tennis. This is more important than tennis," she said, "Also, you can talk to him about town water."

"I'll come!" I said.

Mr. Dee and six prospective constituents arrived promptly at eleven o'-clock on the appointed day. Marjorie brought us all coffee and three dozen hot sugared donut holes, traditional for such get-togethers.

"I think I could do a good job," said the candidate, "I'm a bit of a beginner at this sort of thing. I've spent most of my life laboring in the vineyards at TIME."

"Ah," I mumbled, "backward tumble sentences 'til reels the mind."

He gave me a straight look and changed the subject. Everyone chatted amiably for awhile. No issues or opponents were mentioned.

I blundered into the conversation. "Are you running unopposed or something?"

"No, no," said Marjorie, "he's running against Mr. Dum."

We ate some more donut holes and sipped some more coffee. Finally there was a pause in the friendly conversation.

"What does your opponent stand for?" I blundered in again.

"I don't propose to indulge in character assassination."

"Don't assassinate him, just tell us what he stands for."

"I don't think I'll go into that."

200

"Well, what do *you* stand for?"

"I'm not going to say."

"You won't say what you stand for. You won't say what he stands for. And you won't say when you will say anything."

He munched on a donut hole. "One thing I will say. We're all honorable men. Not a breath of scandal has ever touched our town governing bodies," he said.

I gnashed my teeth silently. Finally in frustration I asked, "Well, if Mr. Dum happened to stand, hypothetically, for unlimited business expansion, do you oppose that idea?"

"I don't say that he's for such a thing."

"But, say he *is*, hypothetically."

"Ah, hypothetically. Well, hypothetically I wouldn't say that I was completely *for* unlimited business expansion. *But* I wouldn't say I was against it either."

I gnashed my teeth more loudly.

"Look," he said. "I know I'm the underdog here. My opponent has 600 votes in his pocket before he even says a word.

"It didn't do him any good last time," mumbled someone.

More random chitchat took place.

"Any questions?" asked the friendly candidate, looking at his watch.

With determination I butted in again. "What would you do about our Water Department? One of the selectpersons told me that the whole board was unhappy with this department."

"Well, first," he chuckled, "I'd vote to put a filter between the pit on Route 28 and Bob Vickrey's house (general laughter). No, seriously, though," he said relaxing, "I think perhaps the situation might be looked into— maybe. In fact, there's some talk of *appointing* the Water Commissioners instead of electing them."

"Are you for *that*," I asked.

"I won't say at this time whether I am or not. What's that grinding sound?"

"That's just Bob gnashing his teeth," said Marjorie hastily, "Now I want to thank Mr. . ."

"Wait," I said, ducking a dirty look. "I have another question. Do you think the selectpersons should make property evaluations for tax purposes? After all, many of them over the decades have been unqualified."

"Two select persons are qualified," added someone.

"Yes, but should they take all that time away from their real jobs to do something that should be done by a paid expert?"

"Selectm—er—persons take a course to qualify for this."

"How long does this course take?" I asked.

"Eleven days," said Mr. Dee.

"We *really* have to break up now," said Marjorie firmly.

"I hope I've answered all your questions," said Mr. Dee cheerfully as he handed out some cards.

"I think it went quite well," said Marjorie after everybody had left.

"I guess that Mr. Dum's meetings were quite similar," I said, "You have to figure out by indirection and innuendos what these people stand for. Also, what are we going to do with 32 donut holes?"

Later that night, I read one of Mr. Dee's cards. He was committed to:

• Improved Public Communications.
• Affordable Housing.
• The Open Space Concept.
• Ground Water Management and Pollution Controls.
• Fiscal Responsibility.

He left out Motherhood, I thought to myself. I guess that means that Mr. Dum vaguely, partially, and hypotheticallly, is committed to:

• Poor Public Communication
• Unaffordable Housing.
• The Closed Space Concept.
• No Ground Water Management and Pollution Controls.
• Fiscal Irresponsibility.

The statement at the bottom of his card read:

If you have questions about any of my positions or qualifications give me a call at ....

Tweedle Dee

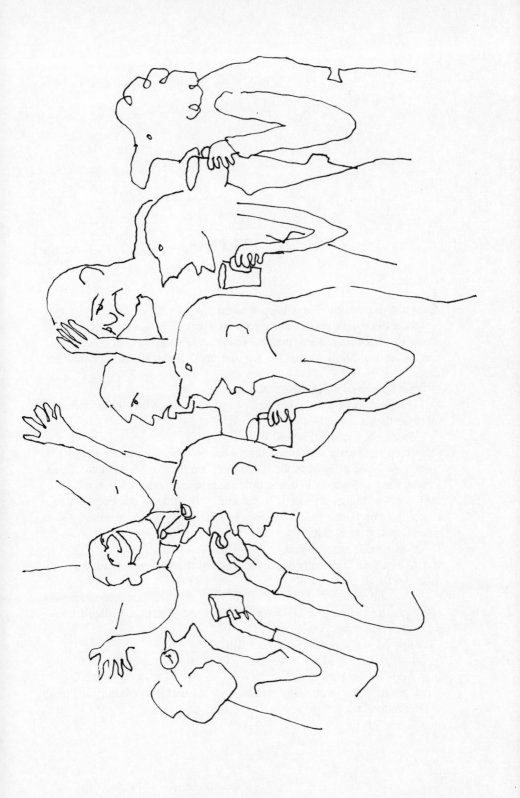

KEY BEEPERS

Lots of interesting things happen in art galleries these days. Recently I was there discussing grave matters with my agent, Bill, when a good looking woman with a voluminous purse walked in. A few minutes later the air was rent by several shrill sounds. "Oh, shut up!" she said abruptly into her purse.

What have you got in there?" I asked.

"That's my key beeper," she replied. "It helps me to find the keys among all these things."

"What gets it going?" asked Bill.

"I clap my hands four times, but it has to have a certain rythym. I'll show you." She clapped to the rythm of "One Potato, Two Potato, Three Potato, Four." Sure enough, the little mechanical monster began to chirp. "All sorts of things activate it," she said. "High heels clacking on tiles, nearby electronic equipment, another key beeper in the same room. Also, when it gets near expensive jewelry."

"It has good taste," I said.

"And *music*! That really excites it. The last time I went to a funeral, the sound of the organ set it off."

"What did you do?" I asked.

"I just looked around like everyone else and pretended I didn't know where the noise was coming from."

"How do you turn it off?" asked Bill.

"It stops after a while," she said. "Oops, there it goes again. It's my high heels on the hard floor."

"It seems to be saying 'Buy one, buy one'," said Bill, tactfully clapping his hands to get it going.

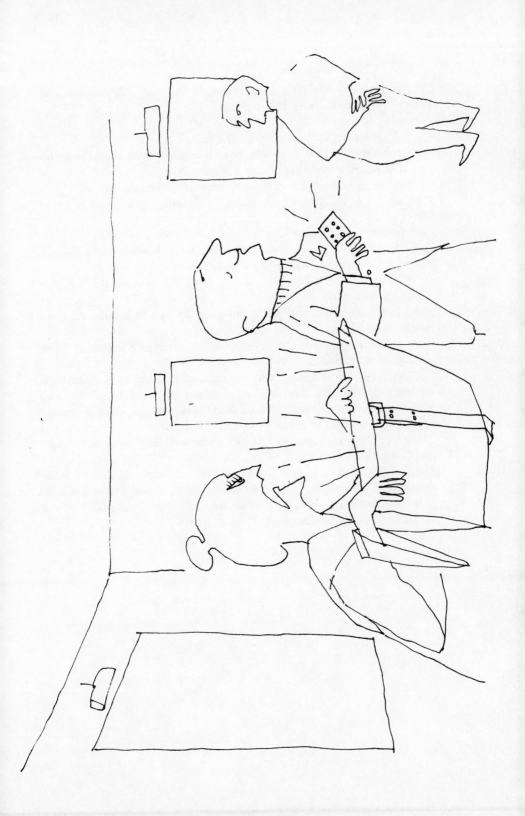

"No. No. You haven't got the rythym," she said. "Remember, One Potato, Two Potato, Three Potato, Four."

Nothing happened.

"Sometimes it's temperamental," she said.

"Let me try," said Bill, coming near. It began to beep almost in terror. "I haven't even clapped yet," said Bill, puzzled.

"Do you have electronic equipment on you?" asked the woman.

"Only my credit-card-size calculator," said Bill, as his pocket began to squeal.

"They're setting *each other* off," she called above the din.

Bill backed away and the noise ceased. Just then a handsome man entered. His briefcase erupted noisily. The woman's purse began again.

"You must have a beeper in there," said the woman. Bill's pocket calculator went crazy.

All this *really* happened, but at this point I began to hallucinate about how it all might end.

"Isn't there some way we can stop this?" called Bill above the noise coming from his pocket.

"They seem to be flirting with each other," I called back, "Maybe if we left them alone together they could work it out themselves." The two beepers calmed down a little, but Bill's calculator became more desperate.

"Oh, no. It wants to get into the act," he shouted.

We took the two gadgets into the next room and placed them on the sofa. They immediately fell silent.

The man and woman spent a considerable amount of time looking at the paintings. Eventually they picked up their two beepers and left, arm in arm.

Bill approached the sofa with a puzzled air. "Hmm," he said. "Where did all these little baby key beepers come from?"

RESISTENTIALISM

T HERE'S a new word in use these days. It's "Resistentialism." It seems
to mean "the tendency of machines to resist the desires of humans." It does
not seem related to the philosophy of Jean Paul Sartre.

Marjorie went to the hardware store recently to buy a new toaster.

"You're lucky," said the salesman. "We have only *one* left. It's won
all sorts of prizes. Even a moron could make a perfect piece of toast."

"Mmm," said Marjorie.

"Yes, it does all your thinking for you. It has a built-in computer, settings
on the bottom, a sliding scale on the side. You can't go wrong."

Marjorie brought it home. She described its wonders and glories to me.

"Great," I said sitting down. "Let's have some toast."

She came back a few minutes later.

"Here's your . . . toast," she said.

"It looks like a piece of warm bread,"

"The toaster refuses to make it any darker."

"Nonsense, just pop it down twice."

"Well . . . I tried that. It doesn't seem to want to."

"What do you mean *it* doesn't want to?

"Well, I mean it *won't.*"

"I know," I said. "We'll set the dial on the bottom for dark, and the
knob on the side for dark. Then we'll watch it carefully and take out the
toast when its just right."

"I have to go to a League of Women Voters meeting," said Marjorie
hastily.

"Don't worry. I can handle it," I boasted.

"Don't get too upset now," said Marjorie as she left.

I read the instructions. "Always place first piece of bread in slot marked 'place first item here', check dial on bottom and knob on side." I did so. Gingerly, I placed two new pieces of bread into the dark slots and depressed the handle. It hummed cheerfully.

Then black smoke poured out. I tried to press up the handle. It whirred angrily, but would not relinquish its victim. I tried again. Clanking sounds greeted my efforts. I opened the front and back doors of the house as smoke filled the kitchen. Finally it sighed contentedly and released two thin cinders.

I got two English muffins from the refrigerator. I put them into the *proper* slots in the *proper* order with the *proper* computer settings. Ten seconds later the machine popped up my icy English muffin. I tried to depress the correct handles. Angry whirring sounds assaulted my ears. The muffins would not stay down. I got a pile of heavy books and arranged them so that *they* would hold down the handle. The machine fought back. Sparks shot out. Banging and growling sounds rent the air. I pulled out the plug in desperation. The machine glowered.

After a while I started to use my fuddled brain. Perhaps a certain amount of time must elapse before popping the muffin down for a second try. There were *four* slots, and I was trying to make *two* English muffin halves.

I plugged it in and started again. When I pushed down my four muffin-halves, it grated angrily and forced them right back up. I took the muffins out and placed them in different slots. Perhaps the toaster had a "memory". No luck!

I always heeded the warning, "place first item here" next to the most smoky slot. Maybe a certain time lapse must occur.

I read a book for five minutes before I tried again, placing muffins in all four slots. Again no luck. I unplugged it and plugged it in again, trying to outwit it. I placed it on its side, thinking that it might work on a gravity principle. I tried two *new* muffins in case it had memorized the original muffin's contours and consistency.

Next I tried the mathematical approach. It seemed to be "willing" to keep the muffins down for about seven seconds. I figured that if I read a book with one hand while I pushed the handle down every seven seconds, in about ten minutes I would have my muffins.

My right hand (especially my main painting finger) became sore. I switched to my left hand, changing the muffins to different slots after each try. Finally my tennis elbow incapacitated me, and I gave in. The toaster glowed with triumph. I put my battered muffin in the oven and soon it was cooked to perfection.

*   *   *

"How did it go?" asked Marjorie when she returned.

"Not too good," I said, "Take the thing back to the store."

"O.K.," she said.

At dinner that night, she told me the news.

"The man at the store says it's the best toaster ever made. He says it's much smarter than we are". He says we can take it to Yarmouth to be repaired."

"Take it," I said.

"I didn't want to hurt his feelings," she said some time later, "Also it'll take several weeks."

"Take it," I said quietly.

A few weeks later, Marjorie brought it back.

"The man insists there's nothing the matter with it," she said. "He says we're doing something wrong. He only charged us $18.50, his minimum price."

"O.K. Let's give it a try. This time *you* do it!"

Marjorie was no more successful than I was.

"They won't take it back," said Marjorie sadly. "They say the toaster is perfect. They say it's . . ."

"Yes, yes, I know, a prize winner. Look, we'll take a loss. Go back to the store and get the cheapest, simplest, junkiest toaster they have. We don't want *any* computer with *any* memory. We want a plain old *dumb* toaster."

"I really couldn't do *that*," said Marjorie, "The man was *so* nice."

"O.K. *I'll* do it," I said.

The salesman was quite upset, but he finally located a simple out-of-date old machine. It makes perfect toast on the first try. We pop English muffins down twice. Once again life is serene.

"What will we do with our beautiful computerized, prize-winning toaster?" asked Marjorie. "Oh, I know, we'll give to Sean. He's a genius with machinery."

"Good thinking," I said.

The story isn't over yet. Sean put the thing with some other items on our front porch and left to get his truck to carry them to his house. While he was gone, the garbage collector took everything by mistake. When we notified his office of this, he agreed to give us two years of free garbage service.

Serendipity!

PROBLEMS, PROBLEMS

I USUALLY paint in egg tempera, a technique in which the pigment is mixed with a combination of egg yolk and water. Many people confuse this with Japanese deep-fat frying. "Tempera, not tempura," I tell them—to no avail. I have other problems, too. For instance, I can't use Cape Cod water. It's too full of acid, iron and other unmentionable things. Recently I've been straining tap water through a gadget called the "Waterthing", which I order from Ohio. It consists of a metal cylinder packed with charcoal and other filtering agents. I pour our dubious town liquid in at the top. Fine, clean water emerges from the bottom. The process takes several hours, though. This instrument has been used by our astronauts (in memory of Dr. Strangelove) to recycle their Precious Bodily Fluids. That's good enough for me!

Disposal of the unwanted egg white has always been a problem. How many meringues, angel-food cakes and daiquiris can one family consume? Our refrigerator filled up with jars full of this slimey material. We tried to give it to our friends. Then I read that Andrew Wyeth has solved the problem by pouring this nutritious substance over his dog's food to guarantee a glossy coat. I tried this on our dog Webster and received (over the uneaten meal) the dirtiest look ever exchanged between beast and man. He ate someplace else for the next few days.

Eventually I realized that egg tempera itself was edible. It happened that I was painting a portrait in a not-too-fastidious apartment. The sittings took place near the kitchen. Each morning I found that the previous day's work had mysteriously disappeared from the panel like the weaving in Penelope's web. It took me a while to realize that the cockroaches each night were eating the day's handiwork. My solution: put it in the refrigerator. I wonder what Leonardo and Michelangelo did.

Finally, a few years ago, I had a small mouse in my studio who became addicted to titanium white. Each morning, when I came to work, I would notice that all of this color had been eaten off my palette. I was puzzled for awhile. Then I noticed him sitting on the floor watching me from about three feet away. He was a perky little fellow, though a bit anemic-looking. His beady eyes betrayed his desperation. His paws trembled. He looked a bit like Peter Lorre. When his craving became too great, he would crawl up the leg of my table *while I was working*, survey the smorgasbord of delicacies, and start munching shakily on a large helping of this favorite drug. No matter how vigorously I shooed him away or sought to lure him to one side with cookies and Life Savers, the minature titanium-white junkie would sit on the floor, glaring at me until I again became absorbed in painting. Then he would scuttle up the table leg once more and head for his "fix." Sometimes I would prepare an extra portion just for him before I left at night. I was beginning to feel like a pusher.

It was hard on his digestion, too. One night I left some Tums on the table. By the next morning he had eaten the whole package. I've never heard a mouse burp, but it must have been pretty noisy behind the wallboards that night. As the months went by the tiny fellow's droppings became pure white, like rice. Before he "O.D.'d", the whole floor was covered with them.

It looked as if there had been some kind of crazy wedding in my studio.

ART SMART

I HAVE a business advisor, whom we'll call Herb. He tries to keep me out of trouble in the dark thickets of commercial enterprise that surround the unwary artist.

"When do I have to get this form in?" I asked in a recent session.

Herb looked at his wristwatch. "Oh, no, not that soon," I gasped.

"I was looking at the calendar on my watch," said Herb, "You have three days.

"And how much do I have to come up with?" I asked.

Herb played with his wristwatch some more. "My calculator says—" and he named an astronomical figure.

"I seem to be paying out a lot of money and getting very little back," I said.

"Trust me," he said. "You'll come out way ahead in the long run. By the way, I've decided to invest in art. I just bought a sporting print by (name deleted on the insistence of my lawyer). It's really beautiful. The gallery owner said it would be a great investment and should go up in value just like a good stock."

Our dialogue continued as follows:

BOB: Don't even good stocks go down sometimes?
HERB: Well, yes, but they go up again—eventually. Anyway, this man said it was an "original" print.
BOB: I happen to know about that artist. He doesn't make those "original" prints. He has his paintings transferred to silk screens by mechanical means. All he does is sign the finished product.
HERB: But it was a *very* reputable gallery. I can't believe they'd gyp me.

212

BOB: They didn't. The whole art world is all loused up these days. Most prints are *not* made by the artists themselves. They hire chromists or photographic specialists to make them. Under their *own* direction, of course. Sort of like the Chairman of the Board of General Motors directing his Vice-Presidents what to do!

HERB: But that's terrible.

BOB: (playing Devil's Advocate) Why?

HERB: We business men think of artists as, well, as loners. People of great, you know, integrity, working away at something they really like. Not worrying about money and all that. My partner has a *signed* Norman Rockwell print. A beloved figure like Rockwell would never get involved in that sort of scheme.

BOB: I happen to know a chromist who made a lot of those prints. Rockwell never touched a single plate. He *did* sign them himself, though, just before he died.

HERB: Well, there you are. The signature is the valuable part. That's what counts.

BOB: What if the artist signs a blank piece of paper—and later someone else prints in the image?

HERB: Ridiculous. That could never happen.

BOB: It did, though. With Salvator Dali.

HERB: (testily) Where did you hear such rubbish?

BOB: I read it in the *New York Times*.

HERB: Anyway, at least it was Dali's signature. That's the important thing.

BOB: Do you like Picasso's work?

HERB: No, but it certainly would be a good investment. A growth stock you might say.

BOB: Would you buy an "original" Picasso print?

HERB: As long as it was signed.

BOB: Suppose it was made three years ago?

HERB: Preposterous! Picasso's been dead for a long time. Even *I* know that.

BOB: I know a kid just out of art school who was making signed Picasso prints three years ago. All perfectly legal.

HERB: But who signed them?

BOB: It isn't quite clear, but evidently it's his granddaughter whose signature looks just like Grandpa's.

HERB: O.K., O.K. But at least in the field of painting we know what's an "original."

BOB: Do we? Andy Warhol has a "factory" of assistants who produce much of his work. His methods have been written up in hundreds of newspapers.

HERB: Who's Andy Warhol?

BOB: You mean you never heard of him?

HERB: (with hurt feelings) Well, can you give me the name of the world's most famous accountant?

BOB: Touche! Then there's another painter (lawyer deletion again) who's color blind. He designs his pictures, but others paint them in. Adolph Gottlieb, sadly enough, had a stroke in his later years. From across the room he directed his assistant where to place each element in the work.

HERB: I'm going right out and sell that sporting print. And I'm telling my partner to get rid of his Norman Rockwell.

BOB: Wait a bit. They'll probably go up in value—at least for awhile.

HERB: (looking at his watch/calendar/calculator) I have to get back to the real world. By the way, (picking up a paperback book) have you read this big best seller, *Iacocca*?

BOB: (looking at it closely) That's not the best seller *Iacocca* by William Novak. That's another book with the same title written by somebody else in order to cash in on the famous one. You know, you can't copyright a title.

HERB: I really gotta go.

WEBSTER—1970—1986

OUR three-legged dog Webster is no longer with us. He left this world a
short while ago with grace and good humor, though crippled, deaf, and in
pain. Our son Sean held him in his arms while the vet administered the
panacea we all might someday wish for.

Our friend had a full and adventurous life, though—occasionally *too*
adventurous! We used to receive telephone calls at all hours to inform us
that he was once more in the local pound.

"Webster's in jail again," said Marjorie.

"What is it this time?" I asked.

"Rape," said Marjorie.

"He really deserves a stiff penalty—or a medal," I mused.

Sometimes we would hear directly from the neighbors.

"Webster's been here again," said one angry lady, "He's been—mo-
lesting our Mitzi."

"You know," I said, "she must be giving off that scent that no male
dog can resist."

"Mitzi is a *perfect* lady. She wouldn't do such a thing." said the woman
huffily.

"Mmm," I said, "You live across the lake you say?"

"Yes," she said.

"Have you been bothered by any other dogs?" I asked.

"Well, yes, but nobody is as persistent as that Webster."

"But he only has one usable back leg," I said.

"It doesn't seem to slow him up," she said.

* * *

215

The years passed, but his glory continued. I came into the kitchen a short while ago and overheard one side of the following conversation. Marjorie filled in the rest later.

"Yes, Webster Vickrey *does* live here. Of course, right now he's staying with our son Sean," she was saying.

"Well, we'd like to contact him," said a bright female voice. "Where can we reach him?"

"I'm afraid I can't give out that number," said Marjorie.

"Well, Webster Vickrey has just won a very nice prize."

"Oh?" said Marjorie.

"Yes," continued the voice, "he and an escort of his choice have just won a fabulous evening out. A limousine will pick up him and his escort. They will be taken to a world-famous restaurant. After dinner, the limousine will take them to the hottest nightspot on the Cape."

"That sounds . . . wonderful," said Marjorie.

"Yes," said the voice, "truly a night to remember. All expenses paid, of course."

"You know," said Marjorie, "Webster Vickrey is a *dog*."

"That's all right," said the voice without missing a beat, "We'll send the limousine for him and his escort anyway. Somebody filled out the form for him and somebody is entitled to this wonderful evening."

"I think my son filled out the form as a joke," said Marjorie.

"We *always* honor our obligations," said the voice.

We contacted Sean.

"My brother and his wife filled that out," he said, "I'm not sure I want to go through with it."

"Why not?" said Marjorie. "It sounds like fun."

"Don't be naive, Mom," said Sean, "A lot of burglars do this so they can rob your house while you're away."

"But the girl on the phone had such a sweet, sincere voice," said Marjorie.

"Momm. . . ." sighed Sean.

"But they don't know where you and Webster live," said Marjorie.

"Sometimes the Bureau of Motor Vehicles does this so they can get you in a definite place and serve you with a lot of parking tickets."

"Are they after *you*?" asked Marjorie.

"No, but *some* people have hundreds of parking tickets piled up," said Sean.

"In Orleans?" asked Marjorie.

"Mom, I'll have to think about it," said Sean.

"Do it for Webster," said Marjorie. "He's getting so old, and it would give him so many nice memories."

"Okay," said Sean reluctantly, "I'll do it for *him*."

Rest in Peace.

DEJA VU

Recently I was watching a wonderful old movie called *Santiago*. Alan Ladd was the cynical woman-hating hero, Lloyd Nolan the cheerful villain, and an Italian actress, Rossana Podesta (with a Spanish accent) the rebel heroine. The story concerned a soldier of fortune who was illegally delivering arms to guerillas in a small Latin American country. Eventually the plot began to sound suspiciously like the evening news. My fuddled brain began to churn . . .

A lot of films these days are remakes of old classics, using new bankable actors, expensive Zoetrope equipment, and a cost overrun of at least forty million. When these extravaganzas run into trouble, the producers call in "play doctors", who anonymously attempt to improve things. *They* write some of the worst dialogue of all. I imagined a script composed entirely of bad lines from Hemingway, Steinbeck, Odets, Tolstoy, Hilton, Benchley, and many others. It might go something like this:

Scene: Cuba—1898

We see five million dollars' worth of beautiful scenery before the camera pans to the hulk of a burning car. Enter Girl (Sophia Loren with a Spanish accent). She is singing a simple folk melody and playing a homemade guitar. From behind the flame steps our Hero (Nick Nolte if Harrison Ford is not available).

HERO: (sniffing) I love the smell of burning gasoline in the morning. It's the smell of victory.
GIRL: Hey Yankee, why you Americanos come all thees way to our poor ravaged country?
HERO: Moolah!

GIRL: Moolah? I do not know thees . . . moolah?

HERO: Moolah. Money! You know, the green stuff. (He waves a hundred dollar bill.)

Enter the Villain (Gene Hackman if Charles Bronson asks for too much money).

VILLAIN: How I love that green stuff. (chuckles) If money was a woman, I'd *marry* it.

GIRL: My people are simple people. They just weesh to be left alone . . . to sweem, to play, to make love.

HERO: When you talk like that, you should wear more clothes.

GIRL: You male chauvinists make everything dirty.

VILLAIN: (chuckling) She's got you there, buddy.

GIRL: You make me feel so *unclean*. You do not respect women.

HERO: Women! (He snorts derisively.) Throw a dozen of 'em up in the air. I'll take the one that sticks to the ceiling.

GIRL: Who *was* she? *Who* broke your heart?

HERO: What does that crack mean?

GIRL: All male chauvinists are bitter because they have been turned down by a good woman.

VILLAIN: What happened to her Spanish accent?

GIRL: (changing subject) Why, here's my leetle brother.

Enter Noble Child (Ricky Schroder in a black wig)

CHILD: Do not let my beeg sister tease you. We live in bad times. Wicked men rule our beautiful land. The good people, the little people who feed the birds, must fight against them.

HERO: (musing) When I was young, I had a beautiful sloe-eyed mistress. Her name was . . . Idealism.

VILLAIN: Yeah, and now she's just another harlot.

GIRL: (sighing) Thank you, though, my fine Americano. You have brought us a dream.

HERO: No. Just *guns*, for which we expect to get paid.

GIRL: But we have no money.

HERO: (sneering) Money talks. It's the *only* language I understand.

CHILD: We . . . we have nothing . . . but our *ideals*.

HERO: Ideals make me deaf. When money talks, my hearing improves.

CHILD: What is that seal I see on your sleeve?

HERO: This is my old West Point shirt. The seal says, "Duty, Honor, Country".

CHILD: Some people wear fine slogans. Others live by them.

VILLAIN: Out of the mouths of babes. . . . . . .

CHILD: If bad men can band together to do bad, why can't good men band together to do good? (He cries on cue.)

VILLAIN: We cut our way through most of this God-forsaken country, fighting alligators, snakes, mosquitoes. But we got your arms through. Now you Freedom Fighters say you ain't got no money.

GIRL: My simple mind cannot understand all thees politics, but we were told that "lower echelon" government officials illegally steered arms to your terrorist enemies in exchange for hostages. You overcharged them, and the excess was deposited into the Swiss bank accounts of our leaders. Two digits were transposed and it was deposited by mistake into the account of an eccentric millionaire. He withdrew it absent mindedly. Therefore we can not pay you.

VILLAIN: Imagine how she would have phrased it if she could talk our language.

(Shots are heard.)

GIRL: (shouting) The government troops are attacking us.

VILLAIN: Grab those guns, you guys. You can pay for them later.

(Government troops attack. After ten million dollars worth of special effects and stunts they are driven off. The Child lies wounded.)

CHILD: Good men must stand together . . . (he cries) Now I go to a world of good men. . . . See the little people who feed the . . . .

(he dies)

HERO: Give the rebels *all* the guns.

VILLAIN: Wait! They didn't pay for them.

HERO: No, but the *kid* did.

GIRL: Now your eyes are shining!

(Music by John Williams rises.)

GIRL: We have been starved, beaten, tortured, but we are the *people*. They can't down *us*. (Shouting to the troops) Avanti Paisanos.

VILLAIN: Paisanos?

HERO: Now I understand "Honor, Duty, Country".

GIRL: (embracing him) I never kissed a man before. Where do the noses go?

VILLAIN: Hey, time for *that* later.

HERO: You know, the problems of two little people don't amount to a hill of beans in this crazy, mixed-up world.

VILLAIN: It's all a big circus, and the clowns are running the show. Oh, well, there will always be another war.

HERO: Anyway, everything will be settled next week. The American troops will be here. The battleship Maine is coming.

GIRL: Who ordered that?

VILLAIN: Oh, some "lower level" civil servants. The President knows nothing about it.

(Exit all singing *Stout Hearted Men* or rather *Los Hombres Valientes*)

FELLOW TRAVELERS

Scene: The Nouveau Neoist Gallery

(A young woman stands enraptured. A man in his thirties enters.)

HE: (half-aloud) Why, this room is completely empty!
SHE: (sniffing) The emptiness *is* the work of art. The artist is simply taking Le Corbusier's statement to its logical conclusion: "Less is more".
HE: (pompously) That statement has also been attributed to Gropius, Brancusi, Moholy-Nagy, Giacometti, Gaudier-Brzeska, and Mies van der Rohe. . . .
SHE: (impressed) Say, you really know your stuff.
HE: Wait, I'm not finished. It was first made by Robert Browning.
SHE: Do you come here often?
HE: Actually, no. I just like to drop in occasionally to view the "cutting edge" of the art world. I really prefer the old masters like de Kooning and Lichtenstein.
SHE: Well . . . if you're interested in ancient history. (noticing his profile) What critics do you like?
HE: Mostly Hughes and Russel.
SHE: (triumphantly) Aha! The dodo-conservatives. I like the new, young critics like Larsen. She *loved* this white room.
HE: Isn't she the one who camped out in Turrell's man-made Arizona crater.
SHE: Twice.
HE: What?
SHE: She did it twice. She called it "a slow death in the cold and dark; at dawn a resurrection."
HE: I get the same effect when I take my kids camping.
SHE: (quickly) You're married?

HE: Divorced.

SHE: Ah! Anyway Turrell's crater will eventually align itself along such celestial markers as the 18.6-year lunar cycle.

HE: God will be *so* pleased.

SHE: (stamping her foot) I don't wish to continue this conversation.

HE: (eyeing her ankles) You're beautiful when you're angry.

SHE: Male-chauvinist Neanderthal! We Neoists are the most vital force in the art world today.

HE: This stuff is just a rehash of the last two decades.

SHE: Yes, don't you see, that's the point. Neoist art must break with the past.

HE: What do you call the past?

SHE: Anything before 1960.

HE: Of course, my real favorites are Marin and Burchfield.

SHE: Who?

HE: Never mind.

SHE: (looking at his shoulders) What other artists do you like?

HE: Kelly, Newman, Noland. Oldies, but goodies.

SHE: (triumphantly) Ivan Kleon anticipated Kelly by fifty years. Newman and Noland's works look suspiciously like the stuff turned out by the early twentieth century Russians Rosanova and Nicholskoya.

HE: When did you learn that?

SHE: I saw it on TV.

HE: (sarcastically) Her Master's Voice!

SHE: TV can be a great art form. Nauman made a video-tape of (I think) himself saying, the words "lip sync" over and over for more than twenty minutes. And everytime he said them, the words were out of sync with his lips.

HE: What's "lip sync"?

SHE: Lip synchronization, Mr. Dope. The soundtrack was wild.

HE: Sounds pretty tame to me.

SHE: No, no, "wild". You know, recorded without a sync signal.

HE: What's a . . . No, I'm not getting into this one. It's too banal.

SHE: Yes, the new art is *banal* on purpose. Irving says, "Boredom is a useful tool."

HE: Right! The purpose of this work is not to create beauty, but to crack the fortress of the art establishment.

SHE: And the corporate market.

HE: Yeah, artists should have something like the *Wall Street Journal*. We could follow their careers: "Poons down thirty points, Frischl topping off,

Wyeth reliable blue-chip, Schnabel the chartists' dream-configuration—a perfect parabola.

SHE: (Looking at his Cartier watch) Are you on Wall Street?

HE: I can modestly say (like Baruch) "I've made a million for every year of my life".

SHE: (conciliatorily) Maybe you'll get to like "The Shock of the New".

HE: That book should be called "The Dull Thud of the New".

SHE: Some of the Neoists *do* go a bit too far.

HE: (taking her hand) And some of them are . . . really quite good.

SHE: (snuggling up as they leave) You certainly are clever.

HE: Say, I just thought of a perfect name for the art of the 80's. Necrophilia Interruptus.

THE GREAT TIP O'NEILL

"Do you have any free time around December 8th or 9th?" I asked Marjorie.

"I'm pretty busy," she said, "You know, League of Women Voters, etc."

"Well, I'm supposed to go to the unveiling of Tip O'Neill's portrait," I said, "I hope you can come."

"I'll try to work it out," said Marjorie.

We arrived in Washington, D.C., the night before the great event.

"Let's get to bed really early," said Marjorie.

Why?" I asked. "We don't have to be there till 10:30."

"Yes, but you have to get up early and work on your speech."

"It's already been written for me," I said, waving several sheets of paper. "Frank Getlein has come up with a great piece of prose. I can't go wrong."

"What are all those red X's?" asked Marjorie.

"Oh, those are just my agent's deletions".

"And those blue X's?" she asked.

"Well, those are the deletions suggested by Tip's staff."

"And all those pencil X's?"

"Various people have told me that those parts were tactless."

"What's left?" asked Marjorie.

"I'll make something up," I said, "I just hope they get my name right."

Our seven o'clock call woke us up.

"I'll sleep a little longer," I mumbled.

"We've got to hurry," said Marjorie, "You haven't even written your speech yet."

"I'll only be talking to a few people in the Speakers' Gallery. It's no big deal. Wake me up in an hour."

"I thought you had to address a joint session of Congress," said Marjorie.

"No, no, just a few . . .," I said, drifting off.

"It's nine o'clock, Bob," said Marjorie, shaking me, "Breakfast is here."

"Tell them to start without me," I grumbled.

"Please wake up," insisted Marjorie, "You've got to shave and put on a tie."

"If I'd known I had to put on a tie, I wouldn't have come," I said into my pillow.

Well, we finally got to the Capitol. I was *almost* awake. I clutched the pocket containing my speech as we hurried up the stairs in the rain. My knee slipped out of joint, and I stopped to whack it back into place. I limped past several guards who electronically supervised us.

"I wonder if Nancy's little pistol gets through these beepers?" I mused.

"Shh," whispered Marjorie.

We were shown into a large room.

"What is this place?" I asked.

"The House of Representatives," said a handsome elderly man who introduced himself as Ambassador Feldman. He shook my hand and shuffled several small pieces of paper.

"You mean, I have to address all these people," I said loudly, as the Marine Corps Band played *Dixie*.

"Yes," he pantomined, as the band switched into the *Battle Hymn of the Republic*."

"I hope they're not going to play *Marching Through Georgia*, I mused, as I looked through the beautiful program. I was the only one without an "Honorable". But at least they got my name right.

"Don't say anything tactless," whispered Marjorie, "You're *not* addressing the Orleans Water Department." She was ushered back to the row behind me.

I patted the pocket where my speech rested uneasily, as my brand-new shirt collar began to bite into my over-shaved neck.

"These things never start on time," said Ambassador Feldman. His fingers shook as he shuffled his multiple papers, which I now recognized as the introductions to the many speakers. I was the seventh. My new collar seemed to grow tighter. I searched through my long typewritten speech. Only three sentences remained uncensored. The band played several more pieces, making sure that no part of the country was left unplacated.

Finally Tip strode in. Everyone burst into wild and sincere applause. It was clear that he was a truly beloved man. He shook my hand heartily, and the ceremony began.

Reverend J. Donald Monan, Marjority Leader Jim Wright, House Republican Leader Robert Michel, Ways and Means Committee Chairman Dan Rostenkowski, Congressman Edward Boland, and Congressman Silvio Conte all made long and moving speeches. Most of them cried. Mrs. O'Neill was escorted to a crimson curtain behind which my portrait was hidden. After some fumbling, she found the proper cord and unveiled my work.

"You made me look too handsome," whispered Tip.

"You're on next," said Ambassador Feldman, shuffling through his papers and losing his place. He proceeded to the podium and went through the papers once more. Hurray! He found the right one and introduced me! I knocked my leg into place and blundered into the light. An idea formed in my fuddled brain.

"I have here," I said, holding it aloft, "a nice long speech written for me by a professional."

A few groans were heard.

"Don't worry," I continued, "I'm not going to read it. By the time various people got through censoring it, I was left with something half-way between a bumper sticker and a fortune cookie. All I can say is that I've painted Presidents, Cardinals, and Senators, but Tip is my hero. This is my favorite protrait of all! I have only one question. Tip, why is your right hand so deeply tanned while your left hand is so nice and pink? I'm going to guess that you wear a glove on your left hand while playing golf."

"You're right," called Tip.

And I sat down. The band played *Happy Birthday To You*. Mrs. O'Neill leaned over and murmured in my ear, "Thank you for making him look so young."

"Tip is ageless," I replied inaudibly, as the band came to a climax.

After the fine benediction by the Reverend James David Ford, one of the Congressmen's wives came up to me, patted me on the arm, and said, "I liked your speech the most. It wasn't the best, but it was the shortest."

Tip put a heavy arm about me and said, "It's a great portrait. I really like it, Bill."